MW00763031
Sept-Îles
Île
d'Anticosti
...wrence River
Gaspé
Îles-de-la-
Madeleine
PRINCE EDWARD
ISLAND
NEW
BRUNSWICK
NOVA
SCOTIA

Translated from French by Annie Mercier and Jean-François Hamel

Copy editor: Majorie Dunham-Landry
Graphic designer: Josée Amyotte
Layout: Johanne Lemay

All photographs are the authors' except for the following:
p. 10 (Cap-Tourmente): Pierre Lahoud
p. 54 (bittern): Philippe Fragnier, Canadian Wildlife Service;
p. 55 (beaver): MEF; pp. 106-107 and 146 (eider): Léo-Guy de Repentigny, Canadian Wildlife Service; p. 113 (boreal owl): Canadian Wildlife Service;
pp. 182-183 and 187 (murre): Jacky Hébert, ATR Îles-de-la-Madeleine;
p. 187 (seal): Pascal Arseneau, ATR Îles-de-la-Madeleine

Canadian Cataloguing in Publication Data

Hamel, Jean-François

The St. Lawrence: The Untamed Beauty of the Great River

Translation of: Le Saint-Laurent

1. St. Lawrence River 2. St. Lawrence River – Pictorial works.

3. Aquatic animals – St. Lawrence River. 4. Aquatic plants – St. Lawrence River.

I. Mercier, Annie. II. Title.

QH106.2.S35H3513 2000 578.76'4'0222 C00-941516-5

Legal deposit: fourth quarter 2000
Bibliothèque nationale du Québec

ISBN 2-7619-1593-3

The publisher gratefully acknowledges the support of the Société de développement des entreprises culturelles du Québec for its publishing program.

We gratefully acknowledge the support of the Canada Council for the Arts for its publishing program.

We acknowledge the financial support of the Government of Canada through the Book Publishing Industry Development Program (BPIDP) for our publishing activities.

EXCLUSIVE DISTRIBUTORS:

- For Canada and
  the United States:
  MESSAGERIES ADP*
  955 Amherst St.
  Montréal, Québec
  H2L 3K4
  Tel.: (514) 523-1182
  Fax: (514) 939-0406
  * A subsidiary of Sogides Ltée

- For France and other countries:
  INTER FORUM
  Immeuble Paryseine, 3 Allée de la Seine
  94854 Ivry Cedex
  Tel.: 01 49 59 11 89/91
  Fax: 01 49 59 11 96
  Orders: Tel.: 02 38 32 71 00
  Fax: 02 38 32 71 28

- For Switzerland:
  DIFFUSION: HAVAS SERVICES SUISSE
  P.O. Box 69 - 1701 Fribourg, Switzerland
  Tel.: (41-26) 460-80-60
  Fax: (41-26) 460-80-68
  Internet: www.havas.ch
  E-mail: office@havas.ch
  DISTRIBUTION: OLF SA
  Z.I. 3 Corminbœuf
  P.O. Box 1061
  CH-1701 FRIBOURG
  Orders: Tel.: (41-26) 467-53-33
  Fax: (41-26) 467-54-66

- For Belgium and
  Luxembourg:
  PRESSES DE BELGIQUE S.A.
  Boulevard de l'Europe 117
  B-1301 Wavre
  Tel.: (010) 42-03-20
  Fax: (010) 41-20-24

For more information about our publications,
please visit our website: **www.edhomme.com**
Other sites of interest: www.edjour.com • www.edtypo.com
www.edvlb.com • www.edhexagone.com • www.edutilis.com

THE ST. LAWRENCE

Jean-François Hamel and Annie Mercier

THE ST. LAWRENCE

The Untamed Beauty of the Great River

For a Giant Among Rivers

We are not done telling of thee
We barely know thee
Through the many faces of thy legends
And the trials of a long intimacy

Thee who spreads eternity within secret gardens
Who wanders around strings of hamlets
Lined with docks safeguarded by lighthouses

When faraway in the open sea
Thou fill the solitude of cliffs and abysses
Of fathomless proportions

When thou convey serene or stormy flows
Thou defy the darkness below
Burning up in thine own light

We are not done searching for thee
Within the depths of thine estuary
Exiled in thy gulf flirting with the ocean

Thou art a god who remodels a creation
Forever tearing and devastating it
Only to lay it perfect, innocent,
In the fragile heart of a milfoil or a tunicate.

Suzanne Paradis
September 2000

*To Suzanne, Louis-Paul, Lucille and Guy,
who are to us what the Great Lakes
are to the St. Lawrence.*

Contents

Today one can only imagine the fabulous event that cut out the gigantic notch that hems the east coast of Canada and forced its way to lay the bed of the St. Lawrence between the Great Lakes and the Atlantic Ocean.

But what do we really know of the origin and evolution of this seemingly familiar river? We have accumulated bits and pieces of information by the thousands, leaving us with equally numerous questions and the irresistible urge to investigate more deeply. With eyes wide open, let us travel the majestic course of one of the richest natural heritages of North America.

A simple freshwater flow at its source, the St. Lawrence soon collects the waters of many tributaries, from north and south, among them the Outaouais, Richelieu, Saint-François, Chaudière, Saguenay, Manicouagan, Romaine and Matapédia. Thus swollen, it races to complete its giant course. Running northeast, like the cold winds of Québec, it broadens into an estuary at the turn of the Old Capital and eventually reaches colossal dimensions. A powerful mixture of fresh water and sea water, the river plunges to inaccessible depths, forcing back almost to infinity the lines of its hardly visible banks. In a rash of gyres, whirling tides and polar temperatures, its gulf is ultimately made compatible with the neighbouring ocean.

Along its course, the St. Lawrence, which flows at 7,800 cubic metres per second (m^3/s) near Cornwall, 11,500 m^3/s close to Trois-Rivières and more than 17,000 m^3/s near Baie-Comeau, grows in size as each tributary joins it. Moving away from the coasts of the Gaspésie peninsula and the Côte-Nord, the gulf waters skirt New Brunswick, Îles-de-la-Madeleine and Prince Edward Island, and brush against Newfoundland and Cape Breton Island before flooding into the North Atlantic.

The St. Lawrence has proven to be a rare hydrographic system. From river to estuary to gulf, it covers nearly 2,000 kilometres

The Isle-aux-Grues archipelago spreads between the banks of the St. Lawrence, slightly downstream of Île d'Orléans, where the river turns into an estuary.

AT FIRST *glance*

Previous pages: The Îles-de-Bas-Saint-Laurent stand guard in the estuary, not far from Rivière-du-Loup.

The expanse of Lac Saint-François bestows a majesty to the St. Lawrence River.

The black-and-yellow markings of a butterfly brightly contrast with the pastel shades of a lilac.

between Lake Ontario and Cape Breton. With the Great Lakes, it forms one of the largest freshwater basins on the planet. However, neither its size nor its output defines it as clearly as its unparalleled amalgam of physical and biotic factors. Along its coasts, the rushing river has stripped the granitic bedrock, carved monoliths of friable rock, cut tall cliffs from the reddish ground, swept pebble beaches and sand dunes, and milled and shaped mud flats bordered by seagrass meadows. Forms and colours harmonize in a magical fresco, the palette eternally renewed by the vastness and diversity of the subject. Defying an already complex sketch, the waters are alternately strangled and stretched, moulded into lakes, bays and straits, made captive of surrounding grounds or given control of huge flood plains. In the gulf, cold and temperate sheets of water clash violently to form the Labrador and Gaspé currents. These are among the unexpected and spectacular elements that impart an undeniable originality to the St. Lawrence, even from a superficial look at its unstable surface and the contours of its shores.

Beneath it all, the daunting river conceals an unequalled diversity of plants and animals. Terrestrial and aquatic life forms inhabit its fresh, brackish and salt waters. Several thousands of species of plants, invertebrates, fishes, birds and mammals have taken up residence there – some permanent, some temporary. For sustenance, cold and fertile waters provide the nutritive elements that encourage the growth of phytoplankton and zooplankton. This effervescent "soup" clouds the water but ensures the continuous renewal of life in a cycle much too complex to describe here.

It is estimated that the St. Lawrence is home to some 1,300 plant species, of which two thirds are

vascular plants rare in Québec; more than 2,200 species of marine invertebrates; hundreds of species of freshwater invertebrates, including a multitude of molluscs and insect larvae; approximately 364 species of resident or migrating birds; close to 200 marine and freshwater fish species; 26 species of amphibians; 23 species of reptiles; 74 species of terrestrial and amphibious mammals; and 22 species of marine mammals. These estimates will obviously evolve as new studies are undertaken and discoveries made.

Humankind has blended fairly well into this admirable diversity: more than 70 percent of Québec's population reside in the Laurentian valley, and nearly 60 percent of the inhabitants enjoy activities that are linked to the St. Lawrence. Some 5,500 commercial fishermen set out on the fresh, brackish and marine waters, catching approximately 70,000 tonnes of eels, snow crabs, shrimps, herring, plaice, scallops, lobsters, sea urchins, etc., every year, not to mention the 260,000 sport fishermen.

The meeting of men and the St. Lawrence is part of Canadian history: Aboriginal Peoples – Mohawk, Huron, Montagnais, Abenaki, Malecite and Micmac – were the first to take advantage of its resources. Europeans later used it to conquer the land and settle there, several centuries ago. In the accounts of Jacques Cartier, the "Province of Canada" referred to the sector roughly located between Portneuf and Île-aux-Coudres; it was much later that the name came to encompass the whole country, from one ocean to the other. In recognition of "St. Lawrence Day," Cartier gave the name "St. Lawrence" to only one of the many bays of the Côte-Nord, where he and his crew dropped anchor. Largely due to misinterpretation, the use of the name later spread to the gulf, then to the whole river, which had also been dubbed Grande-Rivière, Rivière des morues, France Prime, Rivière du Canada and Mayne River. Samuel de Champlain made "St. Lawrence" the official name in the 17th century.

Today, the St. Lawrence bathes several hundred municipalities of which some 40, including Montréal, Longueuil and Sainte-Foy, draw their drinking water from its bed for the use of approximately half the population of Québec. The St. Lawrence also has considerable hydroelectric potential and is among the busiest waterways.

If one compares the St. Lawrence with other large rivers of the world, the usual criteria of classification are hardly in its favour: its 2,000 kilometres leave it well behind the 6,670 kilometres of the Nile or the 6,570 kilometres of the Amazon; its flow of 12,600 m^3/s compares poorly with the 175,000 m^3/s of the Amazon. These figures do not do justice to the vastness of the St. Lawrence; others demonstrate it. For example, water flows from the Gulf of St. Lawrence at 17,000 m^3/s, approximately 10 times less than the Amazon, but it surpasses the latter in the scale and depth of its flood. The Amazon has an average depth of 10 to 50 metres and a width of two to 60 kilometres; another large river, the Mississippi, is 400 metres to two kilometres wide and nine to 15 metres deep. The St. Lawrence has an average width of one to five kilometres in the fluvial section, 40 to 60 kilometres in the maritime estuary and more than 300 kilometres in the gulf; its depth is 10 to 20 metres in the river, more than 300 metres in the estuary and some 500 metres in the gulf. If the St. Lawrence were to be emptied tomorrow morning, it could hold the waters of 15 of the largest rivers in the world. Does it not propel enough fresh water in 24 hours at the output of the Great Lakes to supply the population of the entire planet for more than 40 days?

Within its vastness, the St. Lawrence provides countless havens for both floating and submerged aquatic plants.

This is a fitting indication of the value of a hydrographic network, which, in addition, shelters thousands of islands – some very large, like Île d'Anticosti and Prince Edward Island, others more modest, grouped into archipelagos like Îles-de-la-Paix, Sorel, Saint-Quentin, Bas-Saint-Laurent, Mingan and Îles-de-la-Madeleine.

Take a look at a map of the world, where the contours of continents take shape on the blue fabric of the oceans. What can be said of the Nile, the Amazon, the Mississippi, the Mekong, the Seine, the Rhine or the Danube? Only a trained eye can make out their thin course over the continent they irrigate. What about the Laurentian giant? It's difficult to miss the notch on the coast created by the St. Lawrence as it dives into the heart of North America. Even on the reduced scale of a map, it bursts out, immense, impossible to ignore.

Boldly advancing into the gulf, Gaspésie's Forillon Peninsula keeps watch at the eastern prow of Québec.

The St. Lawrence took two or three millennia to carve the fantastic monoliths of Mingan with materials dating back some 450 million years.

The red sandstone of the Îles-de-la-Madeleine contrasts with the deep blue of the Gulf of St. Lawrence.

Marine meadows accent the littoral of the St. Lawrence.

Delicate yet resistant, the tuberous water lily (Nymphaea tuberosa) *decorates the shallows of the great river.*

A green frog (Rana clamitans) *resting on a water lily: a fitting image of the marshy habitat.*

Between two tides, a fringe of algae spreads out over the rock, offering refuge to the critters of the littoral.

A tuft of wormwood (Artemisa sp.) draws strange arabesques on the rugged cliffs.

From left to right:
The frilled sea anemone (Metridium senile) *is not accustomed to hanging upside down, but this one seems to enjoy it!*

A fierce predator of marine invertebrates, the haddock (Melanogrammus aeglefinus) *gulps down the St. Lawrence's worms, molluscs and crustaceans.*

The blue mussels (Mytilus edulis) *and the green sea urchins* (Strongylocentrotus droebachiensis) *are regulars along the marine coasts of the St. Lawrence.*

This green sea urchin has fallen into the deadly embrace of a hungry sea anemone.

The Atlantic cod (Gadus morhua) *reminds us of the richness of the gulf and of the insatiable human appetite.*

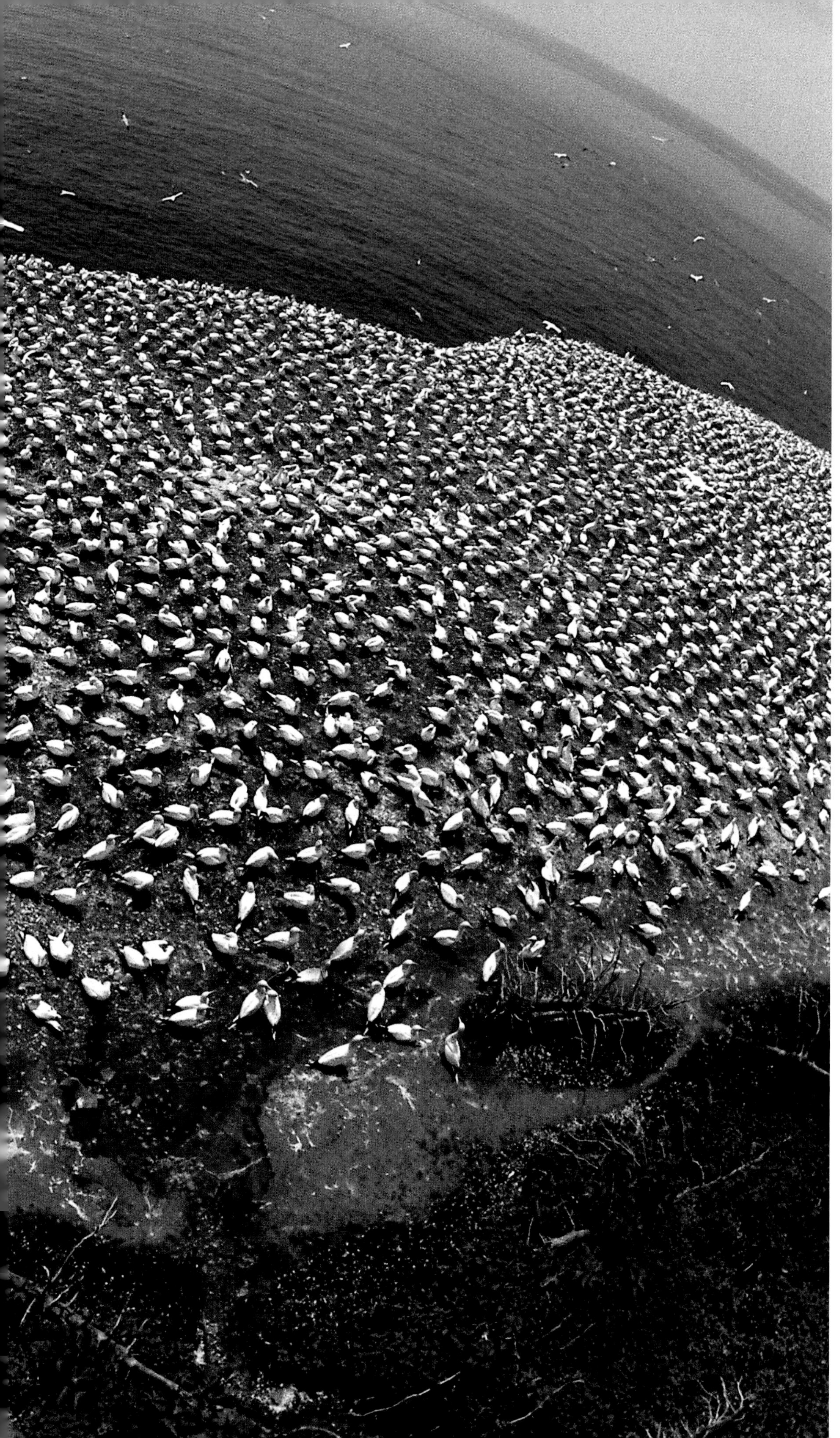

The cliffs that frame the Gulf of St. Lawrence accommodate imposing seabird gatherings, among which is the largest North American colony of northern gannets (Morus bassanus), *established on Île-Bonaventure in front of Rocher-Percé.*

In July, northern gannets feed their young on the rocky headlands of Île-Bonaventure.

Chosen as the emblem of the Canadian 25-cent piece, the mighty moose (Alces alces) *is often observed roaming alongside the ponds and marshes of the St. Lawrence.*

During past centuries, lighthouses have managed the naval traffic of the St. Lawrence; many remain today to keep an eye on passing vessels.

Rowboats and cottages are part of the harmonious setting of the St. Lawrence, as illustrated in this Îles-de-la-Madeleine cove.

VERDANT MEANDERS

The river's first few bends do not reveal its complexity any more than they announce its maritime destination. The budding river merely takes pride in its promising origin as it flows into an already broad bed. Born in Lake Ontario, south of the province of the same name, it peacefully drains the whole of the Great Lakes, one of the largest freshwater reservoirs on the globe. The onset of its race toward the Atlantic creates a liquid border between Québec, Ontario and the United States, all three benefiting from this exclusive opening out into the world. Approximately 200 kilometres from its anchorage point at Wolfe Island, the St. Lawrence is Québec's alone, slicing the province in two, until it spreads majestically around the Maritime Provinces.

There is no evidence of this apotheosis as the river leaves Lake Ontario, except for the striking vision of some 1,800 islands sprinkled across the breadth of the river. Carved by glaciers, now capped with lush vegetation, the Thousand Islands mark the geological transition between the Canadian Shield and the Adirondack Mountains. The islands lie at the very centre of Canadian history. Indeed, Kingston was the capital of Upper Canada during the 1800s. The presence of the islands, together with the narrowing of the river in comparison to the mass of the Great Lakes, offered a migratory bridge to a number of floral and faunal species, enabling them to reach the northernmost areas of distribution. As a consequence, certain plants and trees, such as the deerberry and the pitch pine, and animals like the black rat snake and the least bittern, are commonly found in the Thousand Islands but are rare in other parts of the country.

One can easily understand the popularity of such a cultural and natural paradise. At the turn of the last century, George Boldt, a manager of the Waldorf Astoria Hotel in New York, often vacationed in the Thousand Islands. It was during one of his cruises that Boldt's

The St. Lawrence takes form somewhere between Lake Ontario and the Thousand Islands.

ITS SOURCE, *its resources*

Previous pages: On the border between Canada and the United States, the Thousand Islands offer refuge to myriads of plants and animals.

Upon entering "La Belle Province," the St. Lawrence widens to form Lac Saint-François.

The source of the St. Lawrence River offers a mix of natural treasures and history, which can be discovered in the charming town of Gananoque.

steward, discovering that he was missing some ingredients for his usual salad dressing, improvised a new recipe. Boldt liked the concoction so much that he put the "Thousand Islands" salad dressing on his restaurants' menus and promoted his steward to maître d'hotel of the Waldorf Astoria. Not only did he immortalize the islands in the books of American gastronomy, but the manager of the Waldorf bequeathed a masterpiece of architecture and romanticism to North America: Boldt Castle, built on Heart Island in honour of his wife.

The first human incursions into the Thousand Islands date back to a much more remote period. Traces of a Paleo-Indian culture found on Gordon Island indicate that Natives settled there some 7,000 to 9,000 years ago. More recently, between 700 BC and 1600 of our era, the islands were called Manitouana (Garden of the Great Spirit) by the Iroquois, who set up camps in the area to fish and to smoke their catches in preparation for the winter. A few explorers and famous characters navigated the archipelago, among them Governor Frontenac and Cavelier de La Salle. The latter was concessionary of Fort Cataracoui, renamed Frontenac, known as Kingston today. The confrontations between France and Great Britain, the War of American Independence and the uprising of the Patriots resulted in fortifications and military installations being built throughout the islands. Modern-day visitors have access to no less than 40 archaeological sites commemorating various episodes of the occupation of the Thousand Islands. To the delight of divers, innumerable wrecks lay concealed in the depths. Canadians and Americans peacefully occupy this portion of the river now, sharing the small islands and united in an ecological war against threats to the local environment. On the Canadian side, the St. Lawrence

Islands National Park helps support this battle.

A few kilometres downstream, as it approaches "La Belle Province," the St. Lawrence finally settles, spreading and widening to form Lac Saint-François. This extremely diversified sector of Québec is home to sedge marshes and wetlands that shelter the alder, the willow, the red or silver maple, the American black duck, the green-winged teal, the northern pintail, the lesser and greater scaup, the common goldeneye, the Canada goose and the barred owl. The strange bowfin also hides there. With teeth that resemble those of a beaver, this archaic fish of remarkable voracity is the only survivor of a family known mainly through the study of fossils. Its capacity to breathe atmospheric oxygen makes it one of the rare fishes that can sustain long periods out of the water.

All in all, over 500 higher plants and hundreds of fish and invertebrate species, including several rare varieties, are resisting the attacks of human development, the most frightening being made at the expense of marshy habitats. The presence of many preservation areas, like the Lac Saint-François National Wildlife Area, ensures the reproduction of fish populations and the protection of amphibians and reptiles, and migratory birds that take refuge on the riverbanks during their seasonal voyages. Mammals, too, benefit from a peaceful haven in these settings, in particular the American hare, the eastern chipmunk, the ermine and, Canada's national emblem, the American beaver.

A maze of verdant channels, the south shore of Lac Saint-François shelters most of the plants and animals typical of the St. Lawrence wetlands.

Several meanders of Lac Saint-François are covered in lesser water lilies (Hydrocharis morsus-ranae).

The creeping bellflower (Campanula rapunculoides) *is abundant along the marshes of Lac Saint-François.*

The blueflag (Iris versicolor)*, the floral emblem of Québec, blooms in spring in the intermediate zone between the marsh and the wet meadow.*

Motionless on a cattail leaf, this graceful damselfly awaits its next meal.

The yellow lady's slipper (Cypripedium calceolus)*, another magnificent specimen of the local flora.*

Two Canada geese (Branta canadensis) mirrored in the calm waters of the river.

The common goldeneye (Bucephala clangula) hibernates in the shallow and quiet bays of the river, often looking for protection in the forests that skirt Lac Saint-François.

The cordate pickerelweed (Pontederia cordata) *is a common riparian plant of the St. Lawrence.*

The carp (Cyprinus carpia) *prospers in the soft-bottomed warm waters of the fluvial network.*

The muskellunge (Esox masquinongy) *can measure up to 1.85 m and weigh 45 kg. It is without a doubt among the largest freshwater fishes of the St. Lawrence.*

The horizontal stripes on its chest and large, dark eyes identify the barred owl (Strix varia)*, a noisy nocturnal bird of prey that patrols forested marshes in search of mice, frogs, reptiles and insects.*

This American toad (Bufo americanus) *rests peacefully on the moss-covered shore.*

The eastern chipmunk (Tamias striatus), *a small rodent that frequently visits urban areas.*

This young American bittern (Botaurus lentiginosus) *hides under the abundant cover of riparian vegetation.*

This snowshoe hare (Lepus americanus), *in greyish summer coat, has briefly left the security of the bushes to inspect a neighbouring marsh.*

The imposing dams erected by the American beaver (Castor canadensis) *contribute to the development of wetlands.*

UNEXPECTED OASES

As the St. Lawrence approaches the outskirts of Montréal, human constructions monopolize the view: glass towers and metal piers spread across the harbour. In such an environment, the river becomes merely a waterway for navigation and commerce. At the peak of traffic, people see it mostly as an annoying obstacle between the suburbs and the downtown area or as an element of the city's design.

Its devoted admirers have to close their eyes for a moment to look at it from within, to escape its exterior functionality. Thus the most perspicacious observers have discovered the oases concealed by the port and the highways. They have found that the fauna and flora have not completely deserted the surroundings. In a courageous battle against the ways of the city dwellers, nature has kept an undeniable hold on certain areas. Lac Saint-Louis and Lac des Deux-Montagnes, for example, bathe the natural terrain of Île-Perrot and Îles-Avelle-Wight-et-Hiam, whose maple groves and ponds shelter considerable fauna. The eastern redback salamander, the painted turtle, the green frog and the northern water snake, to name only a few species, have coped with local adversity to find suitable feeding and hibernation grounds. Also present in confined metropolitan habitats is the delicate and vulnerable wild leek. Life thrives on the banks and in the undergrowth, explodes under the waves, safe from the excesses of urban life. Although they have managed to preserve an astonishing richness, the faunal habitats of the metropolitan area have suffered from fragmented territory and human invasion. Conservation and restoration are gaining some ground as the number of wildlife refuges and preservation areas multiply.

Among them is the Îles-de-la-Paix National Wildlife Area, whose name emphasizes the importance of giving some peace to

The natural setting of the shores of Lac Saint-Louis contrasts with the city's concrete structures.

Previous pages: Close to 1,400 merchant vessels come within reach of Montréal each year, confirming the St. Lawrence as North America's key waterway.

The skyscrapers of the metropolis and its suburbs stand out above Lac Saint-Louis as the St. Lawrence lazily slips toward the bridges.

The rounded umbel of the swamp milkweed (Asclepias incarnata) *dominates the dense foliage of the marsh.*

the remaining wilderness. These alluvial low-lying islands could almost be mistaken for a mirage. A central depression has formed a basin where the typical vegetation of the wet plain grows alongside that of the marsh. All around, the littoral displays a kaleidoscopic arrangement in which the gold of the St. John's wort, the four-leafed loosestrife and the cinquefoil mixes with the pink of the milkweed, the flowering rush and the purple loosestrife. The shallows support the growth of horsetails and cattails, while the neighbouring woodlands protect the rare dragon root, a plant that has been listed as a vulnerable species. The American toad, the pickerel frog and the bullfrog find shelter in the wetlands. Significant spring floods force puddle ducks to perch their nests up in the trees, sometimes more than two metres above the ground. Another singularity of the archipelago is the recently established colony of double-crested cormorants, a first in the Montréal area. Other birds, including the tree swallow, black tern, pied-billed grebe, green heron, common moorhen and marsh wren, have set up their breeding and feeding territories nearby.

Other niches for resident and migrating birds have been set aside close to the Ruisseau Saint-Jean, a brook still within the portion of the St. Lawrence that bathes the metropolis. Several ducks have taken to this sector, among them the mallard, the American black duck, the green-winged teal and the wood duck. Profuse vegetation that borders the brook and plentiful invertebrate fauna offer both shelter and food to the muskrats and herons of the neighbourhood. The Ruisseau Saint-Jean is also recognized as the largest fish spawning ground within the flood plain of Lac Saint-Louis. The northern pike, the freshwater drum, the largemouth bass, the pumpkinseed and the brown bullhead breed there every

year. The lake sturgeon, however, colonizes several sites around the islands of the greater Montréal area. The four characteristic barbels of this large fish, which can live up to 100 or 150 years, are designed to locate its prey, all kinds of small, benthic organisms, which are then trapped by its funnel-shaped mouth. The sector hosts the longnose gar, a fish whose reptilian shape evokes a time well before the birth of the St. Lawrence. A little farther downstream, in the midst of the rapids of Lachine, the appropriately named Île-aux-Hérons is a breeding ground for several hundreds of great blue herons and black-crowned night herons. Common terns nest in the vicinity as well. The island is also famous for a fairly uncommon forest assemblage dominated by the sugarberry, a tree that might soon appear on the list of threatened or vulnerable species of Québec. This gem enjoys a particular status in this region: this is its northernmost occurrence.

Beyond the rapids of Lachine and the bridges of the metropolis, the St. Lawrence recovers a certain serenity, at least in the eyes of charmed spectators. The islands around Boucherville are certainly perfect for golf, bicycling and water sports, but more significant tasks occur in these parts, as puddle ducks devote themselves to bringing up their young. The riparian flora and flowering shrubs become a theatre for colourful and melodious exhibitions by cardinals, goldfinches, sparrows, warblers, orioles, chickadees and nuthatches performed for an audience of dancing butterflies. A regular visitor to urban parks, the eastern screech-owl usually nests in a natural cavity, where it hides during the day. At dusk, the raptor comes out to hunt mice, insects, amphibians and birds. Many other members of Québec's fauna make discreet appearances around hikers and cyclists, in broad daylight or at night, as the skyscrapers of Montréal cast their pallid lights on the sleeping sanctuary.

The summer vegetation blossoms into a fantastic explosion of pink and crimson.

An American goldfinch (Carduelis tristis) *in brilliant plumage.*

Although less flamboyant than her male counterpart, the female rose-breasted grosbeak (Pheucticus ludovicianus) *is not without charms.*

Seemingly unconcerned, this great blue heron (Ardea herodias) *stands on the shore, all the while keeping an eye on the prey it has detected.*

The shrill cry of the green frog (Rana clamitans) *blends with the croaking of other amphibians in the metropolitan area.*

This tree swallow (Tachycineta bicolor) *rests for a while before resuming its graceful ballet above the waves in a frantic hunt for insects.*

The double-crested cormorant (Phalacrocorax auritus) *nests on the Îles-de-la-Paix, not far from Montréal.*

Three young mallards splash about under the vigilant gaze of their mother.

Ornithologists often refer to the wood duck (Aix sponsa) *as the most beautiful North American duck.*

The mallard (Anas platyrhynchos), *a common duck of the region's ponds.*

Raccoons (Procyon lotor) *often rummage around shallow banks in search of crayfishes, molluscs and tiny fishes.*

The eastern screech-owl (Otus asio) *nests in hollow trees and occasionally roams around parks and urban areas looking for insects that gather around street lights.*

A small nocturnal rodent, the deer mouse (Peromyscus maniculatus) *makes its home in the Laurentian meadows.*

The male bullfrog (Rana catesbeiana) *can attain 18 cm in length; it is without contest the largest frog on the continent.*

Following pages:
The glimmer of twilight outlines a vessel alongside the sleeping shore.

MAGICAL WETLANDS

Once completely free of the metropolis's grasp, the river lazily spreads out to form Lac Saint-Pierre. It slows down, as if out of breath, its waters becoming trapped within a maze of greenery that draws a fantastic panorama. With a surface area of 480 square kilometres, Lac Saint-Pierre forms the largest flood plain of Québec, encompassing 20 percent of the wetlands of the St. Lawrence as well as several hundred islands. The marshy territory is cut into green ribbons that outline channels and pools, offering a perfect refuge to emergent plants like the cordate pickerelweed, the cattail and the arrowhead. A myriad of invertebrates and fish larvae swim about in a frenzy. Predators and prey mingle as water scorpions, giant water bugs, mayflies, water mites, isopods and pelagic crustaceans stir up the seemingly calm habitat.

Is it wise to let the mystery of the marshes nurture fear or should it not call for a deeper investigation instead? Why are childhood escapades into the marshes so easily forgotten? Almost all children have, at one time or another, waded into a pond in search of tadpoles, frogs and dragonflies to collect and observe. Muddy boots and dirty clothing were of no concern as a parade of bugs whirled, buzzed, burrowed and jumped around the puddles of those summers. Far from frightening or disgusting children, this activity was a continuous source of wonder. Why do the children of yesterday, as they come into adulthood, seem to disregard the magic of dormant waters, which at one time held such fascination?

To all who wish to get back in touch with the wetlands, the St. Lawrence offers countless opportunities. At the crack of dawn, a canoe finds it way through the humid fog that has invaded the river, brushing against the dense vegetation of a ghostly shoreline. A viscous magma adheres to the paddles, adding a faint dripping sound to the surrounding scrambles and choked calls that filter over the tall grasses beyond which gleaming water begins to appear. The

Noteworthy for its diversity of habitats, Lac Saint-Pierre is unique among the wetlands of the St. Lawrence.

Previous pages:
A light breeze ruffles the grasses posted like sentinels on the wet meadow.

The tuberous grass-pink (Calopogon tuberosus) *is a splendid orchid that grows on peat bogs.*

marshy zone slowly but surely reveals its presence. On the banks, dwarf orchids and carnivorous plants, sundews and purple pitcher plants emerge from a spongy carpet of peat moss. Humic acid emanating from rotting plants gives a yellowish tinge to the water, which is almost completely hidden under a tangle of grass and cyperus, creating a floating meadow flanked by ostrich ferns and osmundas, arrowheads and water plantains. Birds and locusts vocalize above this green muddle plastered with glistening spiderwebs. The strange and gloomy call of a common loon echoes in the distance.

In spite of a somewhat discomforting ambience and peculiar odour, the realm of the wetlands is worth a closer look. Water lilies blossom in the shade of bulrushes; pickerelweeds are mirrored on the water's surface, disturbed only by the graceful ballet of a few water striders. Frogs bolt and hide at the slightest whisper. Tadpoles deftly dig up the mud. Backswimmers, water boatmen and great diving beetles slither in all directions. A female mallard solemnly guides her young through the thick vegetal drapes, as damselflies and dragonflies skim the reeds. In the sky above, brown-headed cowbirds, common grackles, kingfishers, ospreys, sharp-shinned and redtail hawks pass by. A red-winged blackbird drives a nosy crow out of its territory. Woodlice, worms and salamanders hide under stumps and decaying tree trunks, even as turtles and grass snakes cautiously leave their own shelters.

All the while, what is occurring in the depths of the marsh? The substrate, a soft and thick silt, is made from the remains of plants, filamentous algae, leaves and branches of fallen trees. Anaerobic decomposition is occurring within the rich layers of soil, generating methane bubbles that rise up to the surface and release a slightly repulsive stench above the quiet wetlands.

Submerged and floating plants benefit from this bacterial activity, which brings them nutrients. Unconcerned by the associated aroma, waterweeds and hornworts proliferate to form gardens of the most luxuriant kind. Rare and translucent wonders of stagnant waters, the freshwater jellyfishes stand out on the green sponges that grow attached to clusters of sunken branches.

The underlying benthic zone offers refuge to several invertebrates, such as worms, sponges, bryozoans and hydras, that reproduce, feed and pamper their eggs there. Ramshorn snails progress head down while devouring decomposing leaves. Thousands of cyclops and cladocerans move restlessly in the company of undulating red worms. Covered in a jelly of frog, snail and fish eggs, pebbles seem to come alive. In the darker recesses, the larvae of great diving beetles and dragonflies patiently stalk tadpoles, invertebrates and small fishes. On the sandy bottom, odd traces indicate the presence of a greenish-brown freshwater mussel: the shell and the foot of this bivalve leave a double furrow on the substrate. Crayfishes and huge leeches also live close to the bottom of the marsh.

Each of the flowers that compose the spike of the cordate pickerelweed (Pontederia cordata) *blooms only for a day.*

The habitats of Lac Saint-Pierre are typical of littoral marshes found in the fluvial sections of the St. Lawrence that are very slightly or not affected by tides. The vegetation comprises a succession of completely submerged or occasionally emerged plants. Common underwater species of this biotope include valisnerias, waterweeds, hornworts and water milfoils. The pelagic section that stretches in the middle ensures the development of freshwater phytoplankton, mainly cryptophyta and chlorophyta, which is sought by the tiny animals of the zooplankton.

The productivity of these marshy habitats makes it possible for a great number of species to live and

The broad-leafed arrowhead (Sagittaria latifolia), so named for the shape of its leaves, grows in fairly dense colonies on the edge of marshes.

proliferate there. Accordingly, Lac Saint-Pierre harbours the largest heron colony of North America. As it searches for a meal, the heron, perched on its long legs, patrols the water or remains motionless, patiently awaiting the coming of a prey to swiftly impale and swallow it before taking position again. Wader birds devour great amounts of fish but also feed on insects and amphibians. They can choose from a wide variety of mudpuppies, eastern newts, blue-spotted, yellow-spotted and redback salamanders, not to

The St. Lawrence skirts the islands of Sorel with an impressive network of channels and marshes.

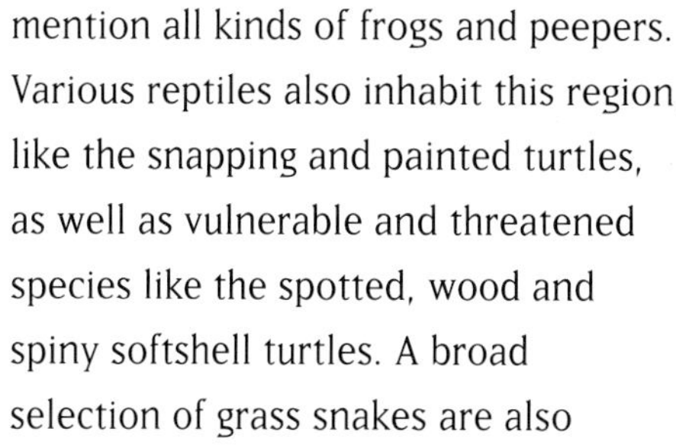

mention all kinds of frogs and peepers. Various reptiles also inhabit this region, like the snapping and painted turtles, as well as vulnerable and threatened species like the spotted, wood and spiny softshell turtles. A broad selection of grass snakes are also present such as the common garter, northern water, brown, smooth green, milk and ringneck snakes.

Fish are not left behind with countless spawning grounds around the islands of Sorel and Lac Saint-Pierre, and nearby Trois-Rivières. Among the familiar ichthyologic fauna are the lake whitefish, the rainbow smelt, the northern rock bass, the yellow perch, the common white sucker, the black crappie, the American shad, the walleye, the channel catfish, the river trout and the Atlantic tomcod. The various substrates, silt, gravel, pebbles or sand, and the submerged grasses, emergent plants and littoral marshes facilitate breeding. The copper redhorse, a fascinating fish endemic to the St. Lawrence and some of its tributaries, has experienced a considerable decline over the last 50 years. Now the only detectable population is in the Richelieu River between Chambly and Sorel.

Thus the St. Lawrence, provider of rich wetlands essential to the survival of hundreds of species, continues to wind its way toward the ocean, still so far away....

A luxuriant blend of tuberous water lily (Nymphaea tuberosa) *and cordate pickerelweed* (Pontederia cordata) *covers parts of Lac Saint-Pierre.*

This fragrant water lily (Nymphaea odorata) *emerges from the amber waters of Lac Saint-Pierre.*

The northern rock bass (Ambloplites rupestris) *feeds mainly at sunrise and sunset.*

The black crappie (Poxomis nigromaculatus) *looks for dense vegetal covers where small insects and fishes abound.*

An island west of Lac Saint-Pierre shelters the most important heron colony in North America.

The sticky tentacles on the leaves of the intermediate sundew (Drosera intermedia) *make for a fearsome carnivorous plant.*

A fierce aquatic predator, the water scorpion secretes a poison that kills the insects, tadpoles and small fishes that fall prey to its attack.

The wood turtle (Clemmys insculpta), *a rare and vulnerable reptile, enjoys a measure of protection around Lac Saint-Pierre.*

The painted turtle (Chrysemys picta) *leaves the marsh in spring to lay its eggs in hollows dug in dryer grounds.*

The snapping turtle (Chelydra serpentina) *has a powerful jaw and a reputation for being vicious.*

This young eastern newt (Notophtalmus viridescens) *seems hesitant at the prospect of abandoning its shelter.*

During the spawning season, the female whitefish (Coregonus clupeaformis) *releases about 25,000 eggs per kilo of body weight.*

Following pages:
The croaking of amphibians and the warbling of birds rock the islands of Sorel to sleep as night falls.

SHORES UNVEILED

The St. Lawrence drifts away from Lac Saint-Pierre to reach the roundabout of the Old Capital. Its flood becomes increasingly powerful as tidal action is more defined. The river is engaging in an unequal duel with the Atlantic Ocean. Oscillations of a few centimetres eventually reach several metres, alternately irrigating and exposing an amphibious ecosystem along shores that are lined with red ash, willow, rough alder and cottonwood. Reeds, emergent and floating plants bow to the flowing river. Local marshes are dominated by American bulrush, flowering rush, wild rice and sedge – a feast for the eyes, a challenge for the imagination! In this region of contrasts, the millennia-old rock of the Canadian Shield sprawls over the lowlands and the boreal forest brushes against the northern deciduous forest. The bulk of the abrupt cliffs bordering the river opposes human intrusion, at least for part of the course.

Under the bridges, aquatic life unfolds in the very wake of heavy naval circulation. Nearly 400 metres of littoral are uncovered twice a day, revealing secret activity. During those intervals, adventurous hikers could journey to the very heart of the river, almost up to the impressive vessels that navigate the seaway. Contrary to general belief, the bottom sediment is neither filthy nor malodorous. Instead, tepid rivulets trickle on fine, compacted mud. Although forbidden to the reckless, the exposed bed of the St. Lawrence is not neglected: great blue and black-crowned night herons leave easily identifiable traces on the humid soil.

The mingling of the tides with the freshwater segment of the St. Lawrence often creates intertidal marshes. Typical vegetation of these marshes is divided into layers that are intermittently exposed and submerged by the daily flood. The lower littoral is rather barren and predominantly muddy. The soft-bottomed middle littoral is frequently covered with American bulrush; wild rice, arrowhead and bur reed grow there as well. This growth attracts tomcods, yellow perch, northern pike and pumpkinseeds. The ebb tide leaves behind a maze of pools and transient marshes that will merge with the river as the flow returns. These improvised oases favour the growth of a multitude of plants, like pondweed, waterweed, water milfoil, and tiny shoots of water plantain and arrowhead. They also give refuge to crayfishes, sponges, freshwater winkles, great pond snails, fragile alevins and insect larvae. A woody vegetation develops on the higher third of the bank. Tidal ponds and creeks irrigated by surrounding brooks are dissimulated under the brushwood. Their surface is almost completely masked by duckweed, frogbits and water shields, in the midst of which sits one of Québec's proudest flowers, the tuberous water lily. Much less popular, battalions of large medicinal leeches lurk underneath. A number of shorelines are dressed with polished tree trunks left by the turning tide; others are padded with freshwater winkle shells that can sometimes pile up to 30 centimetres or more, thus masking the disparate remains of other molluscs.

No matter how invaluable they are, many intertidal wetlands have been filled up and levelled to accommodate highways and bridge foundations. In spite of this human aggression, ponds and artificial swamps persist along roads where aquatic plants proliferate to form sumptuous gardens. These unlikely havens create ideal environments for

UNDER THE BRIDGES *of the capital*

The Québec Bridge can be seen from the riverbank in a quiet Saint-Romuald park.

crayfishes and amphipods that in turn become food for a variety of fishes and birds. Hence, all is not lost in these strange habitats of concrete and asphalt where life sparks every once in a while, though certainly not as profusely as it once did. Long ago, during his second voyage, Jacques Cartier marvelled at Québec's surroundings and the extent of the St. Lawrence waterway. In September 1535, he wrote: "Et remontâmes ce fleuve environ dix lieues, côtoyant ladite île [Île d'Orléans] et, au bout de celle-ci, trouvâmes une fourche d'eaux, fort belle et plaisante, auquel lieu il y a une petite rivière [rivière Saint-Charles]...et trouvâmes que c'était un lieu propice pour mettre nosdits navires en sûreté. Nous nommâmes ledit lieu Sainte-Croix.... Auprès de ce lieu, il y a un peuple dont est seigneur ledit Donnacona, et là est sa demeurance, qui se nomme Stadaconé...."

[And we went up the river about 10 leagues, skirting the island [Île d'Orléans] and at the tip of thee found a pleasing fork in which flowed a small stream [rivière Saint-Charles]...and we found that it was a good place to safely anchor our ships. We named this place Sainte-Croix.... Beyond this place were people whose chief was Donacona and his home named Stadaconé....] (authors' translation)

At that time, no bridge spanned the river. The new settlers had to travel by boat or wait for the river to freeze in order to move from one side to the other. Throughout the 19th century, the section between Montréal and Trois-Rivières was, more often than not, covered with a uniform layer of ice during winter, whereas ice bridges only occasionally formed between Les Écureuils and Sainte-Croix in the Québec sector, or between Île d'Orléans and Côte de Beaupré. The residents of the latter communities frequently had to use ice canoes to push their way through dangerous floating masses. The tradition is vividly revived every year during the Québec Winter Carnival with a boat race that takes place between the frozen shores. This festival, hosted by the cheerful Bonhomme, also renews the rite of crossing the ice bridge to Île d'Orléans. The first permanent structure to straddle the St. Lawrence, the Victoria Bridge, was inaugurated in 1860 between Montréal and Rive-Sud. The Québec Bridge was opened to railway traffic in 1919.

The massive facade of Château Frontenac dominates the river from the heights of the Old Capital.

The American water plantain (Alisma plantago-aquatica) *thrives in the puddles alongside roads almost as naturally as in riparian marshes.*

The emersed pondweed (Potamogeton epihydrus) *possesses both floating and submerged leaves.*

A few kilometres downstream from the capital, just east of Île d'Orléans, the St. Lawrence becomes turbid – grey or brownish in colour – a result of significant physical and biological interactions that are taking place. The river is a powerful conveyor of suspended materials produced by erosion, plankton blooms and anthropogenic emissions, and these materials are responsible for the turbidity. Each year, approximately 2,600,000 tonnes of sediment are carried to Montréal, 4,800,000 tonnes to Trois-Rivières and 6,500,000 tonnes under the bridges of Québec. From an aerial view of

Even though it was only recently introduced in the St. Lawrence, the flowering rush (Butomus umbellatus) *is spreading faster here than in its native Eurasian rivers.*

When the water retreats at ebb tide, the silty strands of Cap-Rouge extend nearly to the heart of the St. Lawrence.

Île-aux-Grues, Grosse-Île and their neighbours, one can see that this cloudiness marks the end of the freshwater monopoly in the St. Lawrence; here, too, the murky river unloads its excess of sediment.

Historically speaking, Grosse-Île, just off Montmagny, served as a quarantine

station for European immigrants between 1832 and 1937. During that period and until World War I, Québec was the primary gateway into Canada. Grosse-Île remembers the tragic year of 1847, when more than 5,000 immigrants, mainly from Ireland, died of typhus.

But aside from its historical significance, the island marks the beginning of a strategic transition in the very nature of the St. Lawrence. The presence of mussel and barnacle larvae confirms that the river and its littoral are slowly metamorphosing: little by little, fresh water is losing its integrity and mixing with the salted vastness of the North Atlantic.

How great it would be to take advantage of the spring thaw, the balmy days of summer or the crispness of autumn and, borrowing the wings of a bird, join the river in its fantastic journey toward the sea!

In order to breed in fresh water, the Atlantic tomcod (Microgadus tomcod) *swims up the St. Lawrence in early winter.*

The American water shield (Brasenia schreberi) *is a delicate yet invasive plant.*

A popular sport-fishing catch, yellow perch (Perca fluviatilis) *often swim in dense schools of several dozen.*

The blackish bulrush (Scirpus atrovirens) *is a grass that thrives on humid ground but does not tolerate submersion.*

Orange hawkweed (Hieracium aurantiacum) *is abundant throughout the St. Lawrence valley.*

Aboriginal Peoples found a way to make a red dye with the latex from the bloodroot (Sanguinaria canadensis)*.*

The delicate forms of the stemless lady's slipper (Cypripedium acaule) *make it stand out among the orchids of Québec.*

An opaque "soup" of sediment stirred up by the river as it surges toward the ocean surrounds the Isle-aux-Grues archipelago.

Grosse-Île is historically famous for being the first port-of-call for thousands of immigrants.

The canoe race presented every year during the Québec Winter Carnival vividly recalls the difficulties encountered by the first riverside residents.

From the heights of Cap-Diamant, the capital keeps an eye on the river year round.

TAKING FLIGHT

Within a few kilometres on both sides of the bridges that connect Québec to the south shore, the intertidal marshes attract a noisy winged fauna. Migratory sanctuaries are abundant everywhere along the St. Lawrence, but the sectors of Pointe-Platon, Saint-Vallier, Cap-Tourmente and Montmagny are particularly busy. American bulrush is plentiful here and the rhizomes of this exceptional grass are on the menu of snow geese. During autumn and spring migrations, these palmipeds invade the bordering marshes. It is believed that their number is nearing the million mark. Indeed, it is believed that the total world population of wildfowl returning from the North halts in the vicinity of Cap-Tourmente in autumn. Whether this is true or not, the banks disappear under the white avalanche that spreads out over the rich mud. Later, the geese's spectacular takeoff offers the opportunity to admire the black tips of their wings and their curved, U formations. These birds cover some 4,000 kilometres at an average speed of 60 kilometres an hour during the spring migration and autumn journey.

No other species causes quite the same stir as snow geese during their feeding frenzy, except perhaps Canada geese, whose loud honking instantly captures the attention of most nearby strollers. Canada geese mainly gather upstream and downstream from the Old Capital, in the marshes and cereal fields of the St. Lawrence valley. In addition to nesting in the Far North, they maintain breeding populations in Québec, from Blanc-Sablon to Île d'Anticosti and around Grandes-Bergeronnes. Sightings of their typical V-shaped formations ritually announce the change of seasons at the spring and autumn equinoxes.

Several other species of shorebirds also appreciate the generosity of the wetlands, particularly plovers, sandpipers,

Snow geese (Chen caerulescens) *assemble for the seasonal migration.*

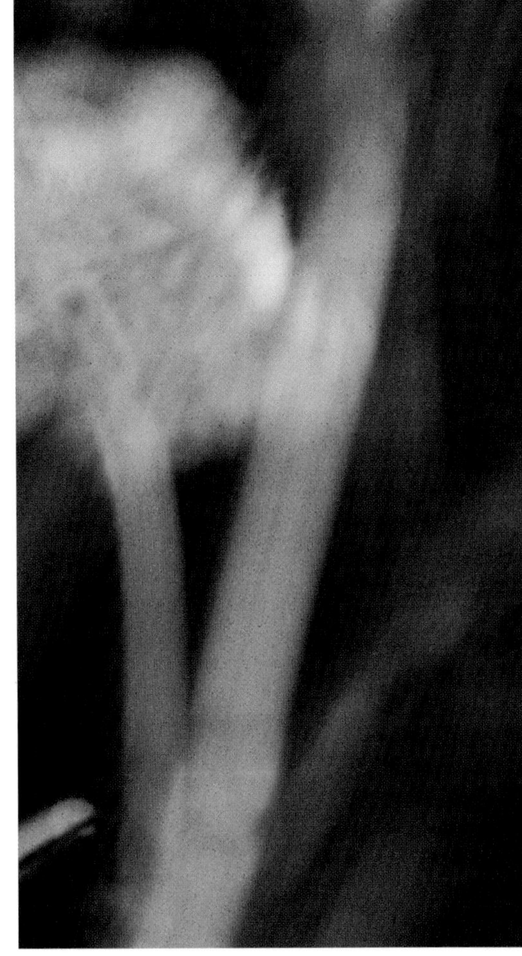

yellowlegs, common snipes and swamp sparrows. Puddle ducks, among them the American black duck, the American wigeon, the mallard and the green-winged teal, nest on the banks more or less peacefully with some 280 other species that visit or take up residence.

Other birds, although more discreet and somewhat precarious, can be observed along the coastal margins of Québec, especially near Cap-Tourmente. Barn owls, Cooper's hawks, least bitterns and peregrine falcons are among the threatened species that can occasionally be seen here. The populations of these species have greatly suffered from the extensive use of organochlorinated pesticides. There are, of course, the more common species, like the red-winged blackbird, the black-capped chickadee, the mourning dove, the blue jay and the assorted varieties of sparrows and warblers. Very common also, the great horned owl generally waits for sunset to exert his hunting skills at the expense of many birds and mammals. Only a lucky observer will have the chance to see the boreal owl as it briefly leaves the cover of the forest to rove out in the open. Winter is the best time to explore the fields and marshes of the littoral in search of the bird of Québec's emblem, the snowy owl, as it stalks hares and ducks. A fearsome diurnal hunter, this bird of prey proudly wears immaculate plumage that matches the icy whiteness of the Canadian Arctic, its main nesting ground.

The clamour and agitation of winged fauna can be seen in several sectors of the river as well, particularly at the beginning of the estuary itself, generally considered to be the eastern tip of Île d'Orléans, where the water begins to have a salty taste. Mammals are also plentiful in these parts. While the muskrat, the otter, the woodchuck and the red squirrel are fairly

common, others, like the red fox, the snowshoe hare, the American porcupine, the raccoon, the American mink and the weasel, are a bit more timid. Perhaps they sense the presence of coyotes, lynx and black bears. Chances are better to see a moose or a white-tailed deer in this vicinity. During summer, only the concert of amphibians competes with the recital of birds, especially at dusk, when the intertidal marshes are veiled in mist. Frogs and toads croon to greet the salamanders and newts as they slip silently out of their hiding places.

From the heights of Québec, a glance eastward reveals the broadening horizon toward which the quickening current of the estuary flows.

Bird lovers cannot resist the plaintive call and subtle plumage of the mourning dove (Zenaida macroura).

The melodious whistle of the black-capped chickadee (Parus atricapillus) *is a familiar sound in Québec.*

A flurry of feathers and water!

The slick black neck and white collar of the Canada goose (Branta canadensis) *set it apart from other migratory birds that seasonally invade the St. Lawrence.*

The American wigeon (Anas americana) *usually builds a nest under a vegetal cover near the water's edge.*

A snow goose (Chen caerulescens) *searches the substrate for roots and tubers.*

The good-natured looks of the snowy owl (Nyctea scandiaca) *hide a merciless predator that hunts birds and small mammals.*

The great horned owl (Bubo virginianus) *regurgitates pellets of bones, feathers and hair that it cannot digest.*

The barn owl (Tyto alba) *can hear the scampering of a mouse from a distance of 30 m.*

The boreal owl (Aegolius funereus) *sometimes leaves the woodland to come into the open.*

A great wanderer, the river otter (Lutra canadensis) *takes a break onshore once in a while.*

The woodchuck, or marmot (Marmota monax), *is frequently seen in the vicinity of the capital and almost everywhere along the St. Lawrence.*

Although the prospect of getting wet is not a favourite of the lynx (Lynx canadensis), *this feline swims well and can hunt down beavers and muskrats in their own territory.*

The adult American porcupine (Erethizon dorsatum) *wears some 30,000 bristles that act as defence weapons or even "floaters" when necessary.*

A lone hunter by nature, the red fox (Vulpes vulpes) *often adds fishes, invertebrates, fruits and plants to its otherwise carnivorous diet.*

Aside from being cute, the red squirrel (Tamiasciurus hudsonicus) *is also provident and takes advantage of summer to store up to 125 kg of food in anticipation of the colder months.*

The muskrat (Ondatra zibethicus) *is a common aquatic rodent that feeds mainly on riparian vegetation.*

The lights go out over the St. Lawrence River and its living treasures.

A PORTRAIT OF THE ESTUARY

As far as the eye can see, metallic dark blue blends with shades of deep green. From Île d'Orléans to the imaginary line that joins Pointe-des-Monts and Capucins, the estuary digests some 400 kilometres of brackish waters as it swallows the river. The icy waves gleam under the caress of the sun. At times, the estuary plunges to more than 300 metres and reaches a breadth of over 60 kilometres. Here lies the largest and certainly one of the coldest estuaries in the world. In spite of four distinct seasons, including a relatively warm summer, the temperature of the water remains near freezing throughout the year, hardly exceeding 2° to 5°C below 10 metres.

Freed from ice some 10,000 years ago, almost at once engulfed by the Golthwait Sea, eastern Québec has been modelled and polished by the hands of time, flooded from east to west by the St. Lawrence, whose rugged shores are now lined with verdant peaks, littoral meadows and sandy beaches. The fauna and the flora of the estuary have slowly evolved into a remarkably diversified ecosystem. Each of the species that successfully adapted to the hazardous conditions has proliferated, forming vast colonies. Hence to protect this natural heritage, portions of land along the estuary have been designated as preservation areas, such as the Parc marin du Saguenay-Saint-Laurent and the Parc de conservation du Bic, as well as the reserves and refuges of Isle-Verte, Île aux Basques and Pointe-au-Père.

Compared to estuaries of other large rivers and probably because of its gigantic proportions, that of the St. Lawrence counts among the most productive hydrologic systems. Even devoid of pollution, its waters retain the same greenish or dark-blue murkiness from one season to the next. Why not the clear turquoise hues of tropical

A flock of birds rises into the clear blue sky of the estuary.

TOWARD *the ocean*

Previous pages: The picturesque cove of Baie-Saint-Paul is among Charlevoix's loveliest scenes.

The Saguenay fjord usually makes quite an impression on those who get a glimpse of its untamed surroundings.

seas? The estuary maintains this murkiness because of an incredible amount of suspended algae and microscopic animals, a richness that the South Seas hardly come close to and can never hope to match. A remarkable food chain thus makes it possible for the St. Lawrence to nourish masses of benthic invertebrates, huge fish populations, thousands of birds and delegations of marine mammals. Among them is the familiar beluga whale, whose white silhouette sharply contrasts with the dark surface of the sea. Fond of caplins, sand lances, cod, salmon, eels and flounders, this comparatively small cetacean can remain underwater for five to 15 minutes and plunge to a depth of 600 metres. Permanent resident of the estuary, the beluga has always excited human curiosity, but it is slowly becoming a living symbol of a much more significant fight.

While nurturing an unmatched faunal kingdom, the St. Lawrence Estuary supports the development of a wide range of human settlements on the picturesque coasts of Charlevoix, Côte-Nord, Bas-Saint-Laurent and Gaspésie. The villages proudly exhibit colourful folklore, each as alive as the river that inspires it.

Snuggled between valleys and vertiginous headlands, the landscapes of Charlevoix have inspired local and foreign artists attracted by the bucolic charms of Baie-Saint-Paul or the old mills of Île-aux-Coudres. The area readily boasts a scar inherited some 350 million years ago from the impact of a 15-billion-tonne meteorite. The natural beauty and cultural richness of Charlevoix have encouraged UNESCO to designate it a Biosphere Reserve. The deep slash of the Saguenay fjord isolates Charlevoix from the Côte-Nord, the latter aligning a succession of maritime hamlets marked by aboriginal influence. The earliest fur-trade post in Canada, Tadoussac has more recently developed pleasant tourist attractions.

Essipit remains just as Champlain described it in 1608, a "petite rivière fort abondante de saumons, où les sauvages y font bonne pêcherie" [a small stream teeming with salmon where Natives make good fishing.] (authors' translation) As Québec's scuba-diving mecca, Les Escoumins offers the discovery of breathtaking marine sanctuaries; Betsiamites is home to a large Montagnais community.

On the southern shore, Bas-Saint-Laurent and Gaspésie willingly share their original treasures. Who has never heard of the woodcarvings of Saint-Jean-Port-Joli, the vestiges of the whale-hunting trade of Île aux Basques, the sumptuous flowers of Jardins de Métis or the tasty shrimps of Matane? In 1762, Bic was the site of the first pilot station, established by locals (for whom the St. Lawrence held no secrets) to help the captains of foreign vessels navigate the treacherous waters of the estuary. The first lighthouse was erected on Île Verte in 1809 and managed by a long line of guardians that ended only in 1988. In spite of these measures, navigation has remained extremely risky, as evidenced by several hundreds, or perhaps thousands, of shipwrecks throughout the 19th century. One of the most tragic occurred off Pointe-au-Père in 1914, when the *Empress of Ireland* went down, claiming the souls of 910 passengers.

It seems that the St. Lawrence Estuary will continue to defy and confuse all attempts at describing its changing moods. Powerful spring tides, deepwater upwellings, and tidal and cyclonic gyres challenge the human imagination by the sheer complexity of their combinations. Add to that polar temperatures, a variable salinity that freshwater infiltrations constantly alter, thick fogs and devastating storms, and the weather forecast is bound to lose credibility. Other movements, such as the currents of Gaspé and Labrador, add to the unreliability of the water masses, not to mention that the daily tidal fluctuations and currents of this section of the St. Lawrence are virtually unpredictable.

Growing on the shore of Métis-sur-Mer, this twisted evergreen bows to a landscape sculpted by the hands of time.

An enchanting landscape transcends the stormy mood of the estuary between Pointe-au-Père and Sainte-Luce on the south shore of the St. Lawrence.

CAFÉ DU MOULIN

The lighthouse of Île Verte is part of the St. Lawrence's maritime heritage.

A northern sea star (Asterias vulgaris) *carries a small daisy brittlestar* (Ophiopholis aculeata) *on its back.*

A storm is brewing to the east of the St. Lawrence Estuary.

From the small village of Notre-Dame-du-Portage, the estuary is rarely more serene and colourful than at sunset.

This humpback whale (Megaptera novaeangliae) *has waded into the estuary in the company of other marine mammals.*

A sumptuous ribbon of islands spreads between the shores of the estuary.

THE LIVING LITTORAL

Like a mighty liquid heart, the estuary beats to the rhythm of an age-old pulse, periodically revealing the intimate treasures of its littoral. Along its vastness, the swaying tides expose the mud flats of Kamouraska as brutally as the rocky coves of Les Escoumins, the polished hills of Bic or the seagrass beds of Pointe-au-Père. The amphidromic point, around which the tidal oscillation revolves, is located at the southwestern tip of Îles-de-la-Madeleine. The wave moves around the gulf in a counter-clockwise rotation, so that high tide in the Cabot Strait coincides with low tide in the estuary. The tide will gradually reach an amplitude of three metres at Rimouski and more than four metres slightly upstream. Ebb tide takes, on average, 12.5 hours to travel from Rivière-au-Renard to Trois-Rivières; high tide takes about nine hours, on average, to cover the same distance. The tidal wave is propelled from Sept-Îles to the mouth of the Saguenay River in one hour; it reaches Québec in five hours and will virtually be lost in Lac Saint-Pierre after 10 hours.

A moving frontier between land and sea, the intertidal zone conceals an unexpected fauna and flora. Alternately submerged and exposed with the to-and-fro of tides, it becomes an oasis for countless critters. The first image that presents itself is often that of large algae wrapped around boulders in a tangle of gleaming moisture, an image comparable to that of long, wet hair. Concealed beneath this apparent mess are translucent green algae lying on a contrasting pink calcareous cover. A plethora of invertebrates that come in all shapes and colours find subsistence among them for a while, or for a lifetime. Scuds, barnacles, periwinkles and limpets are among the most conspicuous. The larger tidal pools of the lower littoral are home to mussels, sea stars, sea urchins and sea anemones in a rainbow of shades.

The estuary carves a vast array of coastal landscapes.

The intertidal area is in perpetual motion, thus creating an unstable and sometimes cruel habitat. As the sea retreats, tidal pools and their denizens are exposed to the whims of wind, sun and rain, not to mention the surge of waves and voracious attacks of seabirds such as ring-billed, great black-backed and herring gulls. With the incoming flow, the ocean reigns once more, exposing the littoral to the appetite of fishes and other aquatic predators.

Attentive scrutiny might reveal a design within this seeming disorder of plants and animals, in particular if the coast presents a marked slope. Life on the shore is often distributed in successive parallel layers. The position of each organism on the littoral depends as fatally on its resistance to desiccation as on the physical characters of its surroundings. Lichens usually occupy the frontier beyond which the habitat becomes terrestrial; there grow the glasswort, the short-liguled ammophila and the beach pea with only a few sea sprays to remind them of the nearby waves. The underlying position is colonized by barnacles, which are gradually replaced by

molluscs like mussels, chitons and limpets. The carapace, or shell, of these animals protects them from the sun during the long hours of daily exposure. Brown algae are among the most fit to resist dehydration. Rockweed, among others, can withstand a major loss of moisture while waiting for the tide to flood it once again. At the low tide mark, red algae dwell in a zone that generally remains submerged and that shelters various molluscs, worms, hydrozoans, sponges and small, mobile crustaceans. Active predators, such as sea urchins, crabs and sea stars, seldom come out of the water; they invade the littoral with the incoming flow, attracted by the abundance of food. Some organisms, the periwinkle, for example, colonize the whole of the intertidal zone. A trained eye will detect many other species, more or less resistant to desiccation, arranged in an order that nature sometimes refashions but never breaks.

As the seasons change, the littoral is the stage of many striking scenes: clam worms twist frenetically, tearing to release their gametes; nudibranchs weave long and lacy ribbons of eggs; barnacle larvae settle into a brand-new generation; scuds swim in pairs for coupling. These moving events preceding the miraculous explosion of life are in sharp contrast with the aggressiveness that characterizes the insatiable quest for food led by the inhabitants of the littoral.

The summer frenzy hardly foretells the rigours of winter in the St. Lawrence Estuary. During the long winter months, a deep sleep will merge land and sea into a hazy, frozen

A scrubby spartina bed adorns the sandy shoreline of Kamouraska.

The rugged hills of Bic roll into the St. Lawrence Estuary.

meadow. It all begins in the tidal pools, where water, chilled and diluted by autumnal downpours, forms a thin layer of ice, imprisoning a mussel or two for the night. Then a white desert begins to stretch toward the sapphire ocean and the turquoise vault of the sky. If spring, summer and autumn are associated with a wild explosion of life, winter seems to spell desolation: the stripped littoral sleeps under snow, soon becoming indistinguishable from the bleak horizon.

Only the April sun and the strong pressure of the tides will break up the ice and carve it into blocks of varying sizes to be carried away by the rushing flow. These frozen monuments will rattle the landscape and brush the coasts, carting tonnes of sand, algae, pebbles and even large rocks trapped at the beginning of winter. Frost will dig scratches and scars into the bedrock, and massive bundles of plants will be swept away. But life will slowly regain control over the barren and distorted substrates as soon as the ice melts. The more vulnerable organisms will not survive, their living conditions having been too brutally modified. Many of them will migrate; others will die. A number of species made captive of the ice will reach remote destinations and thus colonize new sites, where competition might be less ferocious and reproduction more efficient. The coasts that suffer the most from the ordeals of spring thaw are those of the southern bank, where reduced salinity and shallow depths favour ice formation. Downstream, like

The rhizomes of the short-liguled ammophila (Ammophila breviligulata) *help to stabilize the upper littoral zone.*

The great black-backed gull's (Larus marinus) *size and its appetite for invertebrates, fishes and other birds place it among the most formidable coastal predators.*

Who can read the complex history of the Saguenay region inscribed on the tall cliffs of the fjord?

most of the northern coast, the southern shore's constant turbulence opposes the freezing process. The shorelines of many tributaries of the St. Lawrence are similarly shaped by ice and flooding waters over the spring months.

The settings of the estuary are not modelled solely by seasonal rhythms. The coasts are as diversified as they are surprisingly populated. Contrasting with the effervescence of the rocky shores and tidal pools, sand and muddy strands look naked as a desert, although their uniformity is somewhat misleading. Soft substrates are rather unstable; they yield to the subtlest disturbance, which is why the various species that survive in this environment have learned to burrow and hide. Even if they are discreet and inconspicuous by nature, these organisms are no less interesting: sand dollars nestle in the sediment, worms hide in complex underground furrows and display only a crown of showy tentacles. Underneath the plain surface a real kingdom looms, comprising several kinds of clams and other shellfish as well as unusual crustaceans, sea cucumbers and worms covered with a glittery sheath of sand.

This type of milieu, often spread out between the promontories of the estuary, traditionally enjoys a great popularity with visitors. The vast pebbly or sandy expanses attract treasure hunters and shell collectors. Devoid of slippery algae and awkward hollows and hillocks, the seashore exhibits a magical simplicity. Life in these parts is dissimulated so entirely that romantics and collectors must seek attractions of a different sort. Perhaps they see a hidden side to this odd universe that gratifies them with riches from far and inaccessible places! The tide line offers them a fantastic wealth of coded messages: crustacean carapaces and claws, mussel and whelk shells, empty green urchins and sand dollars, seagull feathers, stranded seaweed laced into stunning designs that bewilder or amuse even the most abstracted stroller.

In addition, mud flats are often adorned with strange structures known as "fascines," wood pillars plastered with nets arranged in a V shape and laid out to face the coast. These structures capture migrating eels in the turning tide. A catadromous fish, the American eel lives in fresh water and lays its eggs in the middle of the Atlantic Ocean, more precisely in the Sargasso Sea, off Bermuda. The larvae swim up the Atlantic coast to enter the St. Lawrence, a journey that takes approximately one year, sometimes two. In Québec, commercial eel fishing is mainly carried out near Rivière-du-Loup and farther upstream.

Another model of coastal diversity snuggles inside quiet coves, at the very edge of muddy stretches. As the sea withdraws, alternate-flowered spartina beds are uncovered and gently ruffled by the wind; with the rising tide, they are almost completely engulfed once again. Located higher on the littoral, the meadows of pectinate and spreading spartina are less exposed to tidal movements. The growth of these tall grasses causes fine sediment to accumulate as their root systems stabilize layer after layer of soft substrate.

In addition to bacteria, saltwater marshes of the estuary provide food and a safe haven to a disparate fauna composed of marine or terrestrial visitors, depending on the time of day. Each year, thousands of migratory birds meet in these spartina beds to feast on worms, molluscs, crustaceans and

This jagged cliff covered in seaweed is typical of the north shore near Les Escoumins.

Spartina (Spartina sp.) meadows sway under the caress of the sea breeze.

These fishing apparatuses are deployed inside muddy bays to capture migrating eels.

plants. The eel, the herring and the smelt are occasional visitors as well.

How could we lay out the characteristics of the estuary's littoral without mentioning the Saguenay fjord, whose granite cliffs burst out of icy waters like giant, ageless murals? Even though the most evident spectacle is of a geological rather than a biological nature, by no means does it undermine life. A procession of marine mammals invades the entrance of the fjord each summer, while the intertidal zone accommodates animals and plants typical of brackish shores. Whereas the Saguenay represents a commanding feature of the St. Lawrence Estuary, a good number of enclaves, however remarkable, could easily go unnoticed. Sprinkled near Rivière-du-Loup, the Îles-du-Bas-Saint-Laurent seem to mark the point where the estuary gains in majesty what it has lost of the intimacy of its coasts. Though small, these

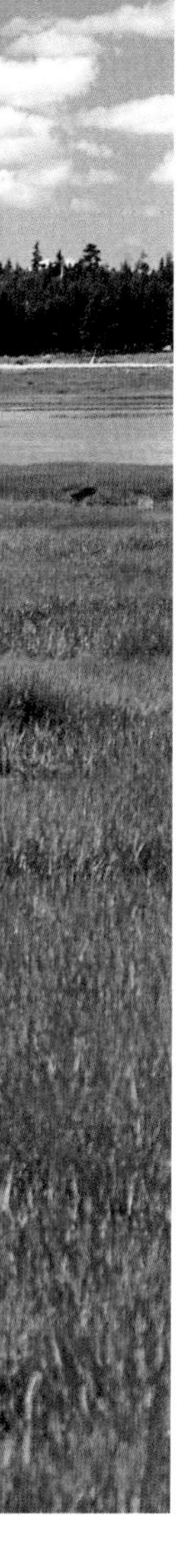

uninhabited islets preserve an untamed and peaceful land as well as a priceless marine heritage. The evocative names of Île aux Lièvres (Hare Island), Île des Pèlerins (Pilgrims Island) and Île du Pot à l'Eau-de-Vie (Brandy Pot Island) testify with humour and accuracy to colourful segments of Québec's history. Several species of birds, such as guillemots, razorbills and the famous eider ducks, visit the coasts of these small islands.

From left to right:
A number of marine invertebrates take cover under the rocks: the sea cucumber (Cucumaria frondosa)*, the common whelk* (Buccinum undatum)*, sponges and sea stars.*

During low tide, bladder rockweed (Fucus vesiculosus) *is stranded along with other intertidal algae.*

A clump of kelp is beginning to show as the tide slowly ebbs.

The rough periwinkle (Littorina saxatilis) *is a small gastropod commonly found on rocky shores.*

As the sea retreats, tidal pools become refuge to numerous plants and animals that live on the littoral.

This small crab has perched itself comfortably on a bunch of algae.

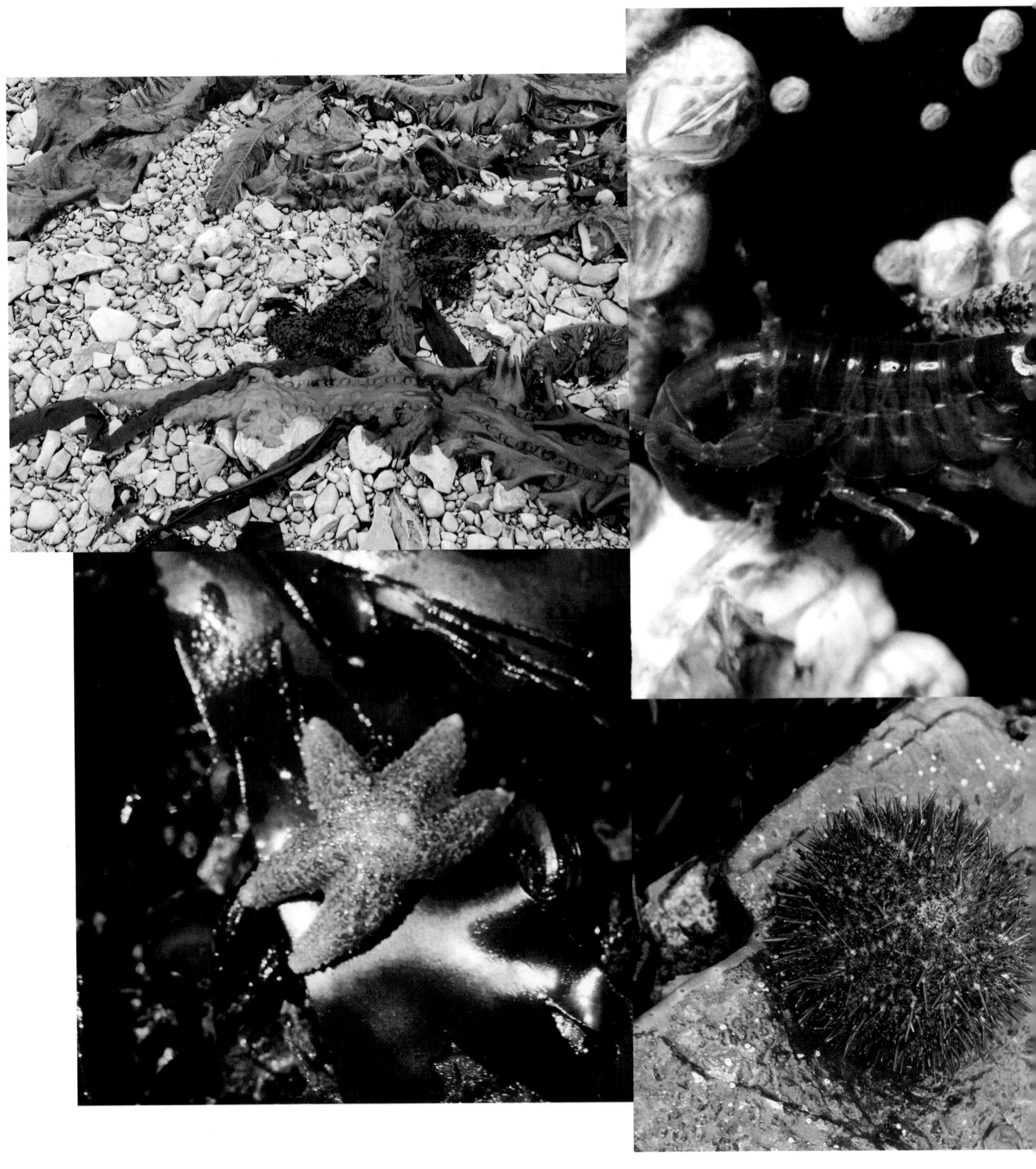

From left to right:
Brown seaweed has been abandoned on a pebble beach by the lowering tide.

The white crests of barnacles decorate the walls of tidal pools where amphipods often swim.

A bed of blue mussels (Mytilus edulis) *and frilled sea anemones* (Metridium senile) *spreads like a living tapestry within the first few metres of the littoral.*

The sea star rarely lets itself get stranded on the exposed shore.

This pair of green sea urchins (Strongylocentrotus droebachiensis) *contrasts sharply with the pink algae-covered boulders on which they rest.*

A sumptuous bed of blue mussels (Mytilus edulis) *borders the littoral zone.*

The riches of the estuary are slowly scattered on the beach by nurturing tides.

The black guillemot (Cepphus grylle) *haunts several coastal islands of the St. Lawrence Estuary.*

A common eider (Somateria mollissima) *nests on a rugged island where members of the species often congregate.*

This female herring gull (Larus argentatus) *broods her eggs on a headland of Île du Pot à l'Eau-de-Vie.*

From left to right:
The fall colours in the vicinity of Bic flamboyantly announce the coming of winter.

At this hour, light and shade are fighting over the estuary's calm immensity.

The impressive ice monuments chiselled over the winter months can have a devastating effect on the littoral during the spring thaw.

Spartina leaves turn yellow as fall spreads over the salt marshes.

Hikers and dreamers roam the shores of the St. Lawrence in search of treasures or peace of mind.

MYSTERY BELOW

The underwater realm of the estuary offers an enlarged and perhaps more complex version of the intertidal universe. Spared the daily cycles of exposure, the sea floor becomes a stable retreat for innumerable marine organisms. Bursting with life and vibrant shades, it makes an extravagant contrast with the even, blue-grey surface of the estuary. Although the temperature is sometimes near freezing within the first 10 metres, soft corals and hydrozoans stretch their delicate, lively shapes on a carpet of pink or brown algae. Every centimetre of substrate is besieged by thousands of growing larvae and hundreds of sponges, bryozoans and tunicates. The dominant species are sea cucumbers, sea urchins and sea anemones that form ubiquitous aggregates, islets of sharp colours in such abundance that they leave divers breathless.

Within the premises of the Centre écologique de Port-au-Saumon and the Saguenay fjord, the water is cold, teeming with phytoplanktonic cells and zooplanktonic animalcules. This is the brackish segment of the St. Lawrence Estuary; surface salinity hardly exceeds 15 to 20 grams of salt per litre of water. The ever-increasing domination of the ocean is announced by the proliferation of sponges, hydrozoans, nudibranchs, sea anemones and giant brittlestars.

However, the fresh water of the river does not yet mix homogeneously with brackish water, such as in the downstream portion of the higher estuary. The surface layer is made of lightly salted, less dense water, and, consequently, it floats over a layer of colder and more saline water. Directly below the surface, in the shallows, the substrate swarms with shrimps, worms and a multitude of molluscs. But sea urchins and other echinoderms, which are susceptible to the slightest variation in salinity, are much less abundant. A few metres deeper, this turbid, poorly salted and rather

The delicate and subtly tinted boreal red shrimp (Pandalus montagui).

tepid sheet rests on a rapidly changing layer: indeed, below 10 to 12 metres, a colder and saltier medium gains in transparency. The fauna becomes typical of quasi oceanic habitats: green sea urchins, polar sea stars, whip- and vase-shaped sponges, arborescent hydrozoans and nudibranchs. Giant brittlestars reign with arrogance, sprawled over soft corals and colonies of hydrozoans that provide anchoring and prevent them from drifting.

It is undoubtedly nightfall that brings out the true splendour of Port-au-Saumon. The planktonic "soup" that clouds the water during the day becomes an incandescent source of light at night. In the St. Lawrence, bioluminescence is mostly related to the activity of certain algae. Agitation "fans" these vegetal cells by increasing the amount of oxygen made available to them. The cascade of metabolic reactions that follows ends with the emission of a greenish sparkle, whose brilliance contrasts with the serene darkness of the surrounding undisturbed waters – a magical and ageless display, able to rid any observer of the concerns that might break the spell! More difficult to make out, other inhabitants lurk in the liquid night. Shrimps, copepods and amphipods that have ventured out into open water frantically converge toward the glow of the projectors, which magnetizes and blinds them. Intrigued by the stir, pelagic predators, octopi or

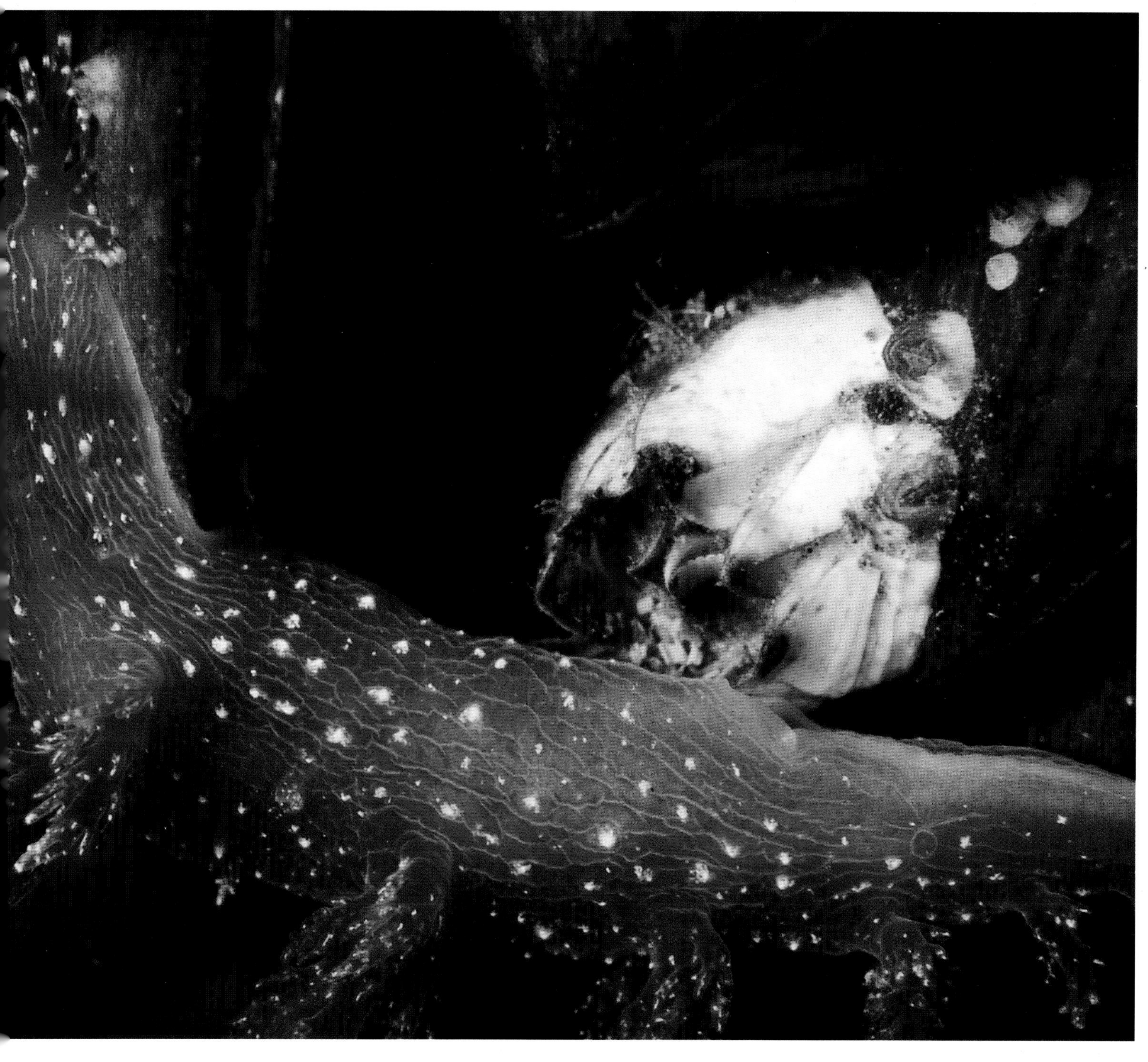

The bushy backed sea slug (Dendronotus frondosus) *is a mollusc devoid of a shell.*

squids, cautiously approach to join in this unexpected feast.

Downstream, around Les Escoumins or in front of the lighthouse of Métis-sur-Mer, the settlement becomes typically marine. Without any concern for order or rank, brittlestars gather in tangled communities to form an incessantly moving kaleidoscope. Tubeworms withdraw at the slightest suspicious movement, hardly showing a glimpse of their

The tentacles of this pair of northern red sea anemones (Urticina felina) *sway with the current.*

These northern sea stars (Asterias vulgaris) *have gathered on a bed of mussels for a feeding frenzy.*

superb plumes. But all are not shy and unsociable in the estuary. The leatherfin lumpsucker, for one, will readily settle on the lens of a camera to show off its bluish glints. As for the sculpin, it often takes to the fins of a diver and tags along for a stroll.

All environments are made of contradictions. Competition and predation prove to be harsh among the populations of seemingly inactive marine invertebrates, but they give rise to the most astounding hunt-and-escape strategies. The behaviour of the sea cucumber, for instance, illustrates the ability of invertebrates to quickly adapt to threatening situations. At the first contact with a predator, this holothurian, which usually makes imperceptible moves, animates and bursts into vigorous contractions that enable it to break free and flee the danger. Another example is the common waved whelk, the favourite prey of the polar sea star. Clutched by the tube feet of its assailant, the mollusc tries to cut loose by vigorously agitating its shell from one side to the other. If this is not enough, it repeatedly strikes the predator with its muscular foot. The polar sea star, whose carefully orchestrated spawning and irreproachable maternal behaviour are worth mentioning, lives exclusively within the cold and fertile waters of the estuary and the Gulf of St. Lawrence.

Other less active but equally effective predators live in the same environment. Northern red anemones occasionally settle at the bottom of rocky cliffs, from which sea urchins tumble down and fall, easy prey, into their arms. The prickly animals are also likely to be swallowed whole by the spiny sunstar.

On the other hand, sea urchins have an appetite of their own: they can trace a devastating path within sumptuous algae gardens. What predator strews sand and mud expanses with hundreds of empty shells? A sea star? Not quite. The small opening found on each hollow shell is the trademark of a gastropod, the northern moon snail, whose attack is carried out in three moves: it digs up the prey, perforates its shell and then introduces its proboscis into the opening to suck the flesh of its victim.

The marine invertebrates of the estuary often fall prey to neighbouring vertebrates. The Atlantic wolffish, for example, crushes green sea urchins in its powerful jaws and swallows their soft tissues. The mackerel, the flounder and the sculpin treat themselves to fast-food meals among the thousands of organisms that spread in undying abundance in their path. Birds gather on the shore to pick up the exposed crabs, clams, mussels, worms and sea urchins that are not armed to argue the choice of a seagull or an eider duck.

Benthic fishes display complex social interactions and are very eclectic in the assortment of their outer appearances: some are flat, others look like tadpoles, porcupines, sticks or round balloons. Champions of camouflage, they can navigate through various substrates without being noticed. The skate, flounder, sculpin, angler, rock gunnel, Arctic shanny, sea raven, wolffish, ocean pout, lumpfish and eel vanish over the sea floor as easily as weasels in a thicket.

Free of any geographical constraints, fishes patrol the estuary at will, venturing beyond the conventional limits of the immense basin. For us, terrestrial creatures with a strict sense of property and a queer habit of delimiting borders, their behaviours are bewildering. Fortunately, the estuary remains free of these concerns. Thus it eagerly overflows to reach colossal dimensions as it pours into the boundary without frontiers of the Gulf of St. Lawrence.

A common rock crab (Cancer irroratus) *is hiding in a cluster of hydrozoans.*

From left to right:
This seemingly lifeless clump is, in fact, an arborescent colony of animals called bryozoans.

With the help of its numerous tube feet, the northern sea star can force open the shells of a mussel and devour its tender flesh.

With a diameter of 30 cm, the northern basket star (Gorgonocephalus arcticus) *is among the largest brittlestars in the world.*

Shapes and colours harmoniously blend in this marine fresco in which a sea star (Henricia *sp.*)*, sponges and calcareous encrusting algae come together.*

Crimson comes to the fore when a spiny sunstar (Crossaster papposus) *meets a tuft of red soft coral* (Gersemia rubiformis).

The Atlantic wolffish (Anarhichas lupus) *usually remains concealed under a rocky shelter, feeding on benthic invertebrates.*

A frequent visitor to the muddy and sandy bottoms of the estuary, the thorny skate (Raja radiata) *owes its name to the thorns that crown its dorsal surface.*

The friendly lumpfish (Cyclopterus lumpus) *can measure up to 45-60 cm.*

The odd-looking ocean pout (Macrozoarces americanus) *has a wide mouth and an eel-like body.*

At the end of a progressive metamorphosis and after having mastered lateral swimming, the flounder's two eyes are on the same side of the head.

FAREWELL TO THE COASTS OF QUÉBEC

Upon leaving Pointe-des-Monts, the St. Lawrence turns into a mighty sea – a sea that the first European explorers mistook for the Atlantic Ocean and only later recognized its limits. An ocean itself, the Gulf of St. Lawrence spreads out over 250,000 square kilometres and has a width of more than 300 kilometres. It bathes a multitude of archipelagos – Sept-Îles, Mingan, Ouapitagone, Sainte-Marie, Petit and Gros Mécatina, Kécarpoui, Saint-Augustin, Blanc-Sablon and Îles-de-la-Madeleine – and embraces the lone features of Île d'Anticosti, Île-Bonaventure and Rocher-Percé. The coastal diversity associated with such magnitude clearly exceeds the breadth of this work. Nevertheless, let us take a panoramic tour of the gulf before saying goodbye to the river that has led us here.

Downstream from Mont-Joli, the Gaspésie peninsula rounds off and advances boldly into the gulf. Inland, the Chics-Chocs and McGerrigle mountains rise to 1,000 metres above sea level. Their windswept peaks shelter the only remaining herd of woodland caribou south of the St. Lawrence. Formerly abundant in these parts, as well as in the Maritime Provinces and New England, the caribou herds were severely affected by logging and human invasion, which forced them to seek protection in the recesses of the Parc de la Gaspésie. Henceforth, the peaks remain the only region in North America shared by three large members of the Cervidae family, the white-tailed deer, the moose and the caribou. Even though the territory is now fiercely protected, the survival of the woodland caribou remains precarious, partly because of the pressure exerted by its predators, the coyote and the black bear. The beast that early Micmacs called *xalibu* (that which scrapes the ground with its foot) has survived and, for the time being, reigns over the mountains of Gaspésie.

The lighthouse of Cap-des-Rosiers looks out onto the gulf's infinite horizon.

GULF WITHOUT *frontiers*

Cap Gaspé is at the easternmost tip of the Gaspésie peninsula.

A tuft of seaweed in its beak, a northern gannet returns to the nest.

In the nearby gulf, the air is crisp, hustled by the winds, and carries the pungent smell of sea spray and guano. Around Île-Bonaventure, the water is sometimes so transparent that one can see the guillemots plunging and gliding under the waves as freely as they fly in the air. Like a living canvas, wet rocks and kelp ribbons are speckled with thousands of tiny mussels, worms and hydrozoans. Sea cucumbers, peaches and anemones match their colours to that of the season. Among the clusters of submerged boulders, various fishes, like the cunner and Atlantic wolffish, play hide-and-seek, while lobsters dance in the undertow. A colossal basking shark skims the surface of the water. Nothing seems to disturb the peace of the gulf or the serenity of the living. Sandy beaches connect to steep headlands over which a myriad of marine birds circle as if on a dizzying carousel between the clouds and foamy waves. Approximately 250,000 nesting birds invade the cliffs of Île-Bonaventure, among them 70,000 northern gannets that form the largest colony of the species in North America. Gracious and skilled gliders, the gannets can dive from a height of 30 metres to capture the herring, mackerel, caplin and squid that make up most of their diet. As they fold their wings to drop on their prey, the magnificent birds transform into arrows and brutally splash into the water.

At the prow of continental Québec, tracing the easternmost tip of Gaspésie, the Forillon Peninsula marks the end of the Appalachian Mountains. The lighthouse of Cap Gaspé guides the sailors who venture into the stormy heart of the gulf. The name "Gaspé" means "where the land ends"; the word is a derivative of the Micmac name "Gespegeoag." But for Jacques Cartier, who discovered it in July 1534 and planted the fleur-de-lys-decorated flag of the king of France, it meant, perhaps, "where the land begins." Lower down, the serenity of the bay of Grande-Grave keeps alive the memories of the fishermen who dried cod on its pebbly beach over a succession of summers. The turn of the

20th century marked the golden days of cod trade under the control of foreign companies. The dried fish were mainly exported to Italy, Spain and the Caribbean islands. Nine thousand years earlier, Native communities benefited from the generosity of the gulf and its wealth of clams, scallops, mussels, whelks, lobsters, shrimps and crabs. The fishing tradition lives on. The scent of cages, bait and boats still permeates the villages of Gaspésie and its Baie-des-Chaleurs. In order to meet the growing demand, a variety of fish and seafood are now farmed thanks to advanced aquaculture techniques, and harvests are being diversified to include new and underexploited fish and invertebrate species, such as the sea cucumber and the common rock crab. The industry and consumers are faced with a sense of urgency, a fear that the gulf might cease to so readily share it vast resources. Hence comes the need to control and eventually proscribe abusive behaviours that are likely to impoverish the coastal waters.

The marine capes of Gaspésie have formed habitats belonging to the late ice age, allowing the growth of plants whose distribution is normally much more northerly. These alpine meadows, limestone walls and screes, exposed to wind and sea, offer refuge to no less than 115 plants of Arctic or alpine affinity. At sea level, the saltwater marshes shelter plants that have adapted to saline conditions and tidal movements. Coastal lagoons are another distinctive trait of Gaspésie, particularly along the littoral of Baie-des-Chaleurs. Locally called *barachois*, from the expression *barre*

Simplicity contributes to the charm of littoral flora.

Scallop harvesting is a lucrative business for the fishermen of the Gaspésie peninsula.

à choir (a barrier to be stranded upon), these formations are mainly made of sand arrows, laid out more or less parallel to the shore at the mouth of some rivers. Good examples of these semi-enclosed habitats occur at Saint-Omer and Carleton, where they ensure the growth of plankton and become home to benthic invertebrates and numbers of small fishes that can tolerate salinity fluctuations. Hence colonies of birds find abundant food in these lagoons.

On the opposite side of the gulf, the Côte-Nord offers an array of untamed scenery: the powdery beaches of Gallix and Moisie, the deep coves of Rivière-au-Tonnerre and the rugged hillsides of Magpie. North of the 50th parallel, the boreal forest fades out to be replaced by stunted thickets and spongy peat bogs where abounds a typical vegetal assemblage composed of cotton grass, marsh marigold, cloudberry and Canadian rhododendron. Upon entering the village of Longue-Pointe, one is drawn by the deep blue of the gulf that surrounds the islands and small islets of Minganie. Silhouetted in the crimson light of dawn or cloaked in mist, the monoliths of Îles Mingan take on the elusive shapes of flowerpots, gigantic human profiles or fantastic ghost ships. Some 35 kilometres to the south sits Île d'Anticosti and its 7,943 square kilometres of green forests, canyons, falls and lakes. Kingdom of the white-tailed deer, the island boasts incomparable natural riches, including the famous Jupiter River, where Atlantic salmon breed in great number every year. The colossal yet timid moose hides amongst the spruces and balsam firs. In March 1881, J.-U. Grégory, who was chief of the Marine ministry in Québec, enthusiastically noted that "l'île d'Anticosti peut être appelée le cœur du golfe Saint-Laurent car toutes les variétés aquatiques, depuis la baleine monstrueuse jusqu'au minuscule capelan, semblent s'y être donné rendez-vous et les rivières abondent en saumons et en truites." [The island of Anticosti can be called the heart of the Gulf of St. Lawrence because all the aquatic life forms, from the monstrous whale to the tiny caplin, seem to have gathered there, and the rivers are teeming with salmon and trout.] (authors' translation)

In addition to fishes and mammals, Île d'Anticosti harbours a well-known

winged emblem: the bald eagle, which also nests elsewhere along the St. Lawrence, preferably at the top of tall trees, more rarely on the ledge of a cliff. Its nest is a bulky cluster of branches and grass that becomes huge over the years with repeated occupations and renovations. The majesty of the large raptor makes up for less dignifying necrophagous practices and the pilfering it commits at the expense of the osprey. The population of bald eagles underwent a significant decline in North America during the last century, but their status in Québec leaves room for hope.

A forceful sea wind brushes the clouds from the sky over the Moyenne-Côte-Nord.

*Following pages:
The lighthouse at Cap Gaspé.*

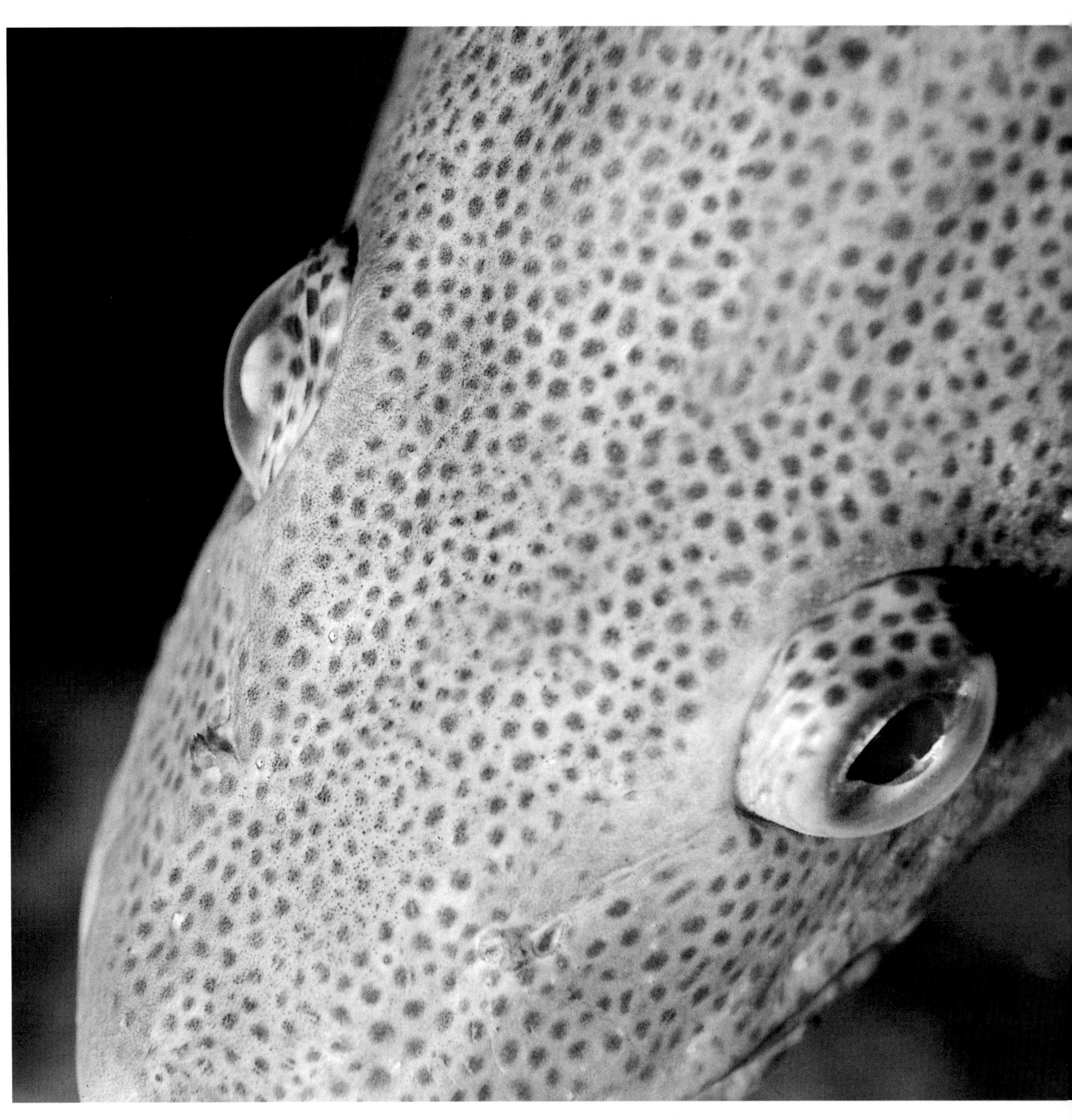

The Atlantic cod (Gadus morhua) *is a commercial species that has been harvested for centuries.*

When the first settlers came, Atlantic salmon (Salmo salar) *were swimming up the St. Lawrence all the way to Niagara; today, the proud fishes continue to breed in numerous rivers of the Laurentian system, including those of Gaspésie, the Côte-Nord and Île d'Anticosti.*

The cunner (Tautogolabrus adspersus) *breeds between June and August in the Gulf of St. Lawrence.*

The pink shrimp (Pandalus borealis), *which measures between 7 and 10 cm, is the most heavily fished shrimp species in the gulf.*

The vicinity of Grande-Grave, in Parc Forillon, has witnessed the passage of countless fishermen and their families.

This view of the Côte-Nord, not far from Baie-Sainte-Marguerite, emphasizes the contrast between the pale, powdery sand and the deep hues of the gulf.

Rocher-Percé is an instantly recognizable landmark of Gaspésie and of the Gulf of St. Lawrence.

Harsh weather coupled with the quiet power of the gulf has sculpted this rocky beach of Minganie.

The elements of nature have carved this colossal sculpture, which rises out of the littoral of Minganie.

The flowering spike of this willow herb (Epilobium sp.) stands before the greyish shores of Île Quarry.

The bald eagle (Haliaeetus leucocephalus), *a majestic bird of prey with a very distinct cry.*

Parc de la Gaspésie shelters the only remaining population of woodland caribou (Rangifer tarandus caribou) *south of the St. Lawrence.*

The white-tailed deer (Odocoileus virginianus) *has conquered Île d'Anticosti.*

The American black bear (Ursus americanus) *leaves a signature that combines sight and smell on the trees of its domain.*

This young moose (Alces alces) *cautiously emerges from the thicket where it took a nap.*

Several specimens of Québec flora present a clever mix of fragility and heartiness that ensures their survival.

Somewhat incongruous on a sandy beach, this vegetal assemblage has caught the eye...of the camera.

In early spring, the Canadian rhododendron (Rhododendron canadense) *is covered with delicate pink blossoms.*

This bucolic landscape of Baie-des-Chaleurs is typical of the region.

MARITIME FLAVOUR

While the river remains viscerally tied to the province of Québec as it slices it in two from east to west, the gulf defines marine territories around Newfoundland, Nova Scotia, New Brunswick and Prince Edward Island. Recalling that Ontario gave birth to the river, a total of six out of the 10 Canadian provinces are connected by this unique stretch of water.

Some 200 kilometres off the Gaspésie peninsula, the Îles-de-la-Madeleine bring a taste of Québec to the middle of the gulf. The combined action of wind, waves and human effort has welded six of the 12 islands of the archipelago into a thin, sandy crescent. When Jacques Cartier reached them in 1534, they were distinct yet formed in a unique alternation of cliffs and beaches, bestowing a majesty to the landscape. At that time, the navigator thus praised Île Brion: "Cette dite île est la meilleure terre que nous ayons vue, car un arpent d'icelle terre vaut mieux que toute la Terre-Neuve. Nous la trouvâmes pleine de beaux arbres, prairies, champs de blé sauvage et de pois en fleurs, aussi épais et aussi beaux que je vis oncques en Bretagne, qu'eux semblaient y avoir été semés par laboureux." [This island is the best land we have seen, because one arpent of thee is better than all Newfoundland. We found it full of beautiful trees, meadows, wild corn fields and blossoming peas, as thick and as beautiful as I saw in Brittany, that seemed to have been sown by a ploughman.] (author's translation)

The Îles-de-la-Madeleine's proximity to the Gulf Stream helps to soothe the harshness of an oceanic environment. Thus their climate is mild and rather windy. The Acadian roots of the population highlight the charm of the archipelago, where fishing still provides the main source of income. In the midst of ruthless winds and storms, the islands offer sanctuary to colonies of marine birds, and harp seals invade the nearby ice floes at the end of winter to give

Nothing else in sight but the Gulf of St. Lawrence.

Previous pages: Isolated in the middle of the gulf among the rest of the Îles-de-la-Madeleine, the Rocher aux Oiseaux is host to huge colonies of migratory birds.

Polished rocks have piled up along the shoreline of Havre-aux-Maisons.

The wind, rain and waves have eroded the shores of the Îles-de-la-Madeleine.

birth. Even the imposing leatherback turtle, a rare and threatened species, stops there on occasion.

At the end of the 16th century, all of French Canada, including southeast Québec, Prince Edward Island, New Brunswick and Nova Scotia, bore the name of Acadie. Whether it referred to the heavenly "Arcadie" of Ancient Greece, to the Malecite *quoddy* (fertile place) or to the *algatig* (camping site) of the Micmacs, the name was probably adopted by the Italian navigator Giovanni da Verrazzano, who explored the sector in the early 1500s. In those days, Acadie also included a good portion of New England. The victory of the British over Louisbourg in 1758 and the capitulation of Québec in 1759 marked the end of the French regime in Canada. The British authorities undertook a massive deportation of the French-Catholic population of Halifax; they had to wait until 1764 before recovering their land, henceforth restricted to a few coastal zones of Nova Scotia and New Brunswick as well as various small isolated communities in the gulf. This traumatic episode deeply scarred the Acadian people, but it did not strip them of their ardent pride nor of the warm intonations of their vibrant speech.

In addition to a colourful history, the coast of New Brunswick brings an exceptional wilderness to light. Miscou Island, for example, presents sumptuous peat bogs covered with scores of pitcher plants and sundews. Another contrasted model of wetlands and sandy beaches extends at the mouth of the Kouchibouguac River, in the park of the same name. At low tide, the sand banks show through the surface, the white crescents of the dunes glittering from afar. The marine labyrinth is criss-crossed with narrow canals and eelgrass prairies. Hundreds of sticklebacks colonize the brackish waters of the tributaries. During summer, these small fishes enter breeding season: the bright-red male makes an assiduous courtship to all females available. The soft substrate accommodates an impressive assortment of shrimps, flounders and molluscs. Hundreds of aggressive gulls and terns nest on the small, sandy islands, rocked by the waves, surveying their eggs among the grasses. The fact that the eggs are laid in simple hollows explains the nervousness of the terns and their attempts at intimidation

A couple of double-crested cormorants (Phalacrocorax auritus) *skim the waves.*

Harp seal (Phoca groenlandica) *pups are born on the ice floes off the Îles-de-la-Madeleine.*

The common murre (Uria aalge) *frequents the Îles-de-la-Madeleine archipelago where it finds plenty of fish.*

against all unwelcome visitors. It may be worth mentioning that this species undertakes one of the most remarkable migrations: the population of eastern Canada crosses the North Atlantic, reaches Europe and flies along the western coast of this continent to reach the southern hemisphere in an extraordinary journey that can cover up to 35,000 kilometres.

A most remarkable bird, the piping plover visits selected dunes and coastal areas of the gulf. Its populations are precarious in North America and in danger of becoming extinct in eastern Canada. This charming bird usually lays its eggs along sandy beaches, which are becoming increasingly popular with swimmers and tourists. During the last decades, many of its breeding territories have been destroyed by urban and tourist development. The dunes that certain parks of New Brunswick, Prince Edward Island and Nova Scotia set aside for the piping plover are its last refuges in the east of the country. Several pairs gather there each year, and remarkable efforts are being made to help them protect their broods against all-terrain vehicles, foxes and seagulls, among other dangers. Their uncertain fate has promoted the creation of many protected zones in Canada and the United States. It is estimated that between 4,000 and 6,000 piping plovers remain today, of which approximately seven percent are believed to frequent the eastern Canadian coasts.

More easily seen and perhaps more ubiquitous because of their size and appearance, Atlantic puffins periodically gather in certain sectors of the gulf: Îles Mingan, Île d'Anticosti and Îles-de-la-Madeleine, the coasts of Newfoundland and New Brunswick, where they lay their eggs in burrows as deep as 50 to 200 centimetres. The contrasted nuptial plumage of the puffin is so different from its sober winter colours that it has long been reported as two distinct species. The Atlantic puffin is an accomplished

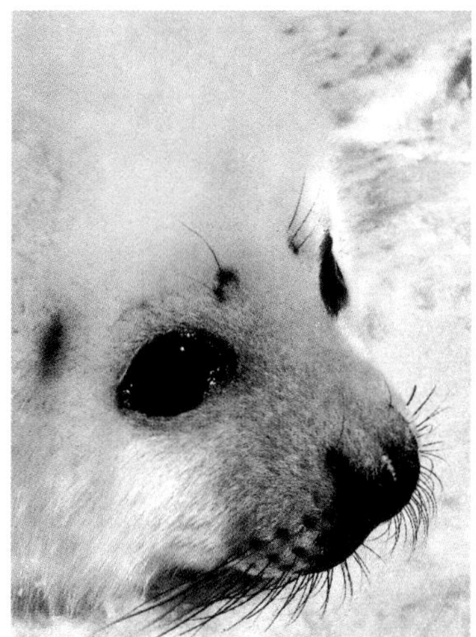

swimmer, but its takeoff and flight are rather awkward, so much so that a landing bird may sometimes collide with a close neighbour. Much steadier in flight, the black-legged gull, or kittiwake, puts up perfectly well with the vastness of the gulf. It prefers the open sea, where it finds plenty to drink, waves to rest on and food to pick at in the wake of fishing vessels. It will only approach the coasts to nest. A vast colony of black-legged gulls occupies Île-Bonaventure; others adopt the northern shore of the St. Lawrence, Île d'Anticosti and the east coast of New Brunswick. In the seagull family, the kittiwake is the only species that dives to capture its food, mainly small fishes and zooplankton. A great traveller, this bird covers incredible distances around the polar circle.

From left to right:
A loud horde of Arctic terns (Sterna paradisaea) *suddenly disperses over the dunes of Kouchibouguac National Park.*

Arctic terns (Sterna paradisaea) *perform impressive migrations that can cover more than 35,000 km.*

The Arctic tern lays its eggs on the sand.

The Atlantic puffin (Fratercula arctica)*, easily recognizable in its colourful plumage, nests on the rocky overhangs of numerous islands of the gulf.*

The greater shearwater (Puffinus gravis) *feeds at the surface of the water.*

Following pages: The New Brunswick village of Belledune has an open view of Baie-des-Chaleurs.

This peaceful harbour welcomes visitors on the Acadian coast of New Brunswick.

The three-spined stickleback (Gasterosteus aculeatus) *breeds at the mouth of many rivers that flow into the Gulf of St. Lawrence.*

Off to sea!

The white hake (Urophycis tenuis) *is a prized commercial species of the Gulf of St. Lawrence.*

WHERE THE GIANTS FEAST

Away from the coasts, the pelagic habitat is mainly populated by infinitesimal beings grouped under the name of plankton. These organisms passively drift with the current and only barely move within a limited scale. From femtoplankton, whose diameter ranges between two hundredths to two tenths of a micrometre, to megaplankton, that can measure several metres across, all planktonic forms evolve in the water column and significantly contribute to the food chains of all marine ecosystems.

Although the greater part of planktonic activity cannot be seen by the naked eye, a number of animals and some of their peculiar behaviours do not fail to draw attention. Among them, the graceful sway of a medusa will not go unnoticed. Jellyfishes are regarded as one of the most imposing planktonic groups. The lion's mane, for instance, has huge members whose tentacles can reach more than 50 metres. Smaller and very delicate, the moon jellyfish resembles a flying saucer. Some jellyfishes will invade the gulf only during specific periods of the year. Among these, hydromedusae are special in the way that they are the reproductive vessels of benthic hydrozoans. When the time comes, they are released as minute umbels, which scatter by the thousands in the open ocean. Squadrons of translucent balloons are sometimes mixed with them and can easily be mistaken for small jellyfishes. Nevertheless, these ctenophores are only close relatives. What a sight they are when sunlight reflects on their undulating cilia and makes them iridescent against the oceanic backdrop!

The bounty of the gulf is well known to marine creatures that gather there each year to feast, usually on their way back from the South Seas. Most of the mammals, from the minke whale to the colossal blue whale, including a parade of seals, dolphins and

A humpback whale dives deep into the St. Lawrence.

porpoises, enter the gulf as soon as the ice breaks up. Several of them continue onward into the estuary, chiefly to plunder the resources of the Saguenay surroundings. The baleen whales seek plankton and schools of small fishes, which they engulf, tonnes at a time, in a spectacular frenzy. Humpback whales, for example, join efforts to gather prey using bubble nets. In the gulf, they feed mainly on herring and caplin. The acrobatic feats of the humpback whales are dazzling: these monsters, weighing 30 to 40 tonnes, can propel themselves out of the water completely, like grotesque rockets, before falling down heavily on their side or back. Some even splash their caudal fin around or rub against one another.

Blue whales come to the gulf, with a preference for the northern coast, between April and December. With a weight of 180 tonnes and a length of 30 metres, they are the titans of the planet. Imagine: a blue whale's heart is the size of a Volkswagen Beetle and is able to pump 10 tonnes of blood through the body; the aorta, the main blood vessel, is wide enough for a man to swim in comfortably! It is not surprising that the blow of this whale spouts nine metres above the water. Nevertheless, the blue giant eats only tiny animals, mainly krill and copepods, but no less than four tonnes a day...of course!

Toothed whales, such as dolphins and porpoises, patrol the gulf on a regular basis, as do seals. Proficient predators, they mostly consume fishes, cephalopods and other marine invertebrates. Agile and fast, they hunt their prey close to the bottom or in open water. The harbour seal is especially fond of calm waters spreading in bays, coves and sounds. In winter, it avoids floes and remains in the sectors that are free of drift ice. It feeds on herring, smelt, squid, char, trout, whitefish, redfish and Atlantic salmon. The grey seal mainly lives around rocky and sandy shores. Able to dive down to some 220 metres, it manages to tear broad openings in fishing nets to steal the catches, thereby helping them to escape. Grey seals are hunted locally along the Côte-Nord close to Les Escoumins, as well as in the Mingan archipelago and around Île d'Anticosti. Among the carnivores, the killer whale enjoys a rather unique position: it frequently attacks other marine mammals and does not fear any natural predator.

The sun shimmers on the dark surface of the Gulf of St. Lawrence.

There are over 20 species of mammals in the seas of Québec and the Maritimes, many of which are found in the Gulf of St. Lawrence, in the Mingan archipelago, close to Île d'Anticosti and around the Gaspésie peninsula: the fin, humpback and blue whales, the minke whale, the Atlantic white-sided dolphin, the harbour porpoise, the grey and harbour seals. The killer whale, white-beaked dolphin, long-finned pilot whale and sperm whale are occasional visitors. At the eastern end of the gulf, Newfoundland occupies a preferred marine-mammal route in the Labrador current. Similarly, to the south, the coast of New Brunswick is visited by many whales, while Nova Scotia receives significant herds of long-finned pilot whales. The outskirts of Îles-de-la-Madeleine are primarily famous for the harp seals that gather on the floes to give birth to their furry white pups.

In addition to familiar fishes and mammals, the gulf welcomes a few unexpected guests, even exceptional ones from the south, most having been driven from their path by storms or attracted by the abundance of food. Among them are the American white pelican, the white shark, the blue shark, the hammerhead shark, the common ocean sunfish, the striped burrfish, the planehead filefish and the grey triggerfish. These visitors from abroad add a touch of exoticism and mystery to an already mystifying marine environment that remains a perpetual source of wonder.

A solitary ammophila (Ammophila breviligulata) *stands on the beach, only steps away from the dense colonies that steady the surrounding sand dunes.*

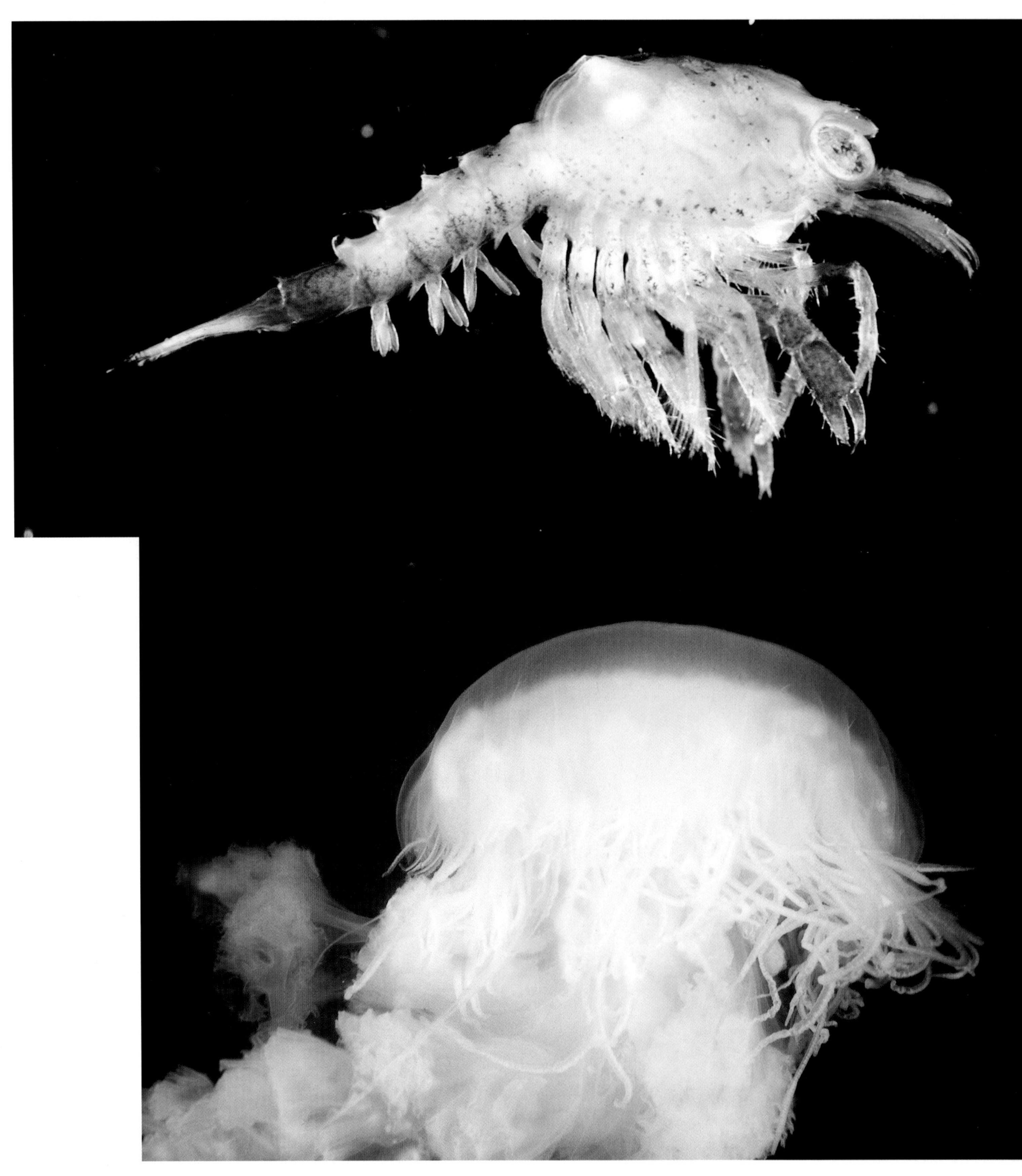

A lobster larva (Homarus americanus) *joins the plankton for a few weeks.*

The lion's mane jellyfish (Cyanea capilata) *is a remarkable member of the zooplankton.*

This graceful hydromedusa – and its reflection – swims along the surface of the gulf.

From left to right:
The tail of the humpback whale (Megaptera novaeangliae) *rises vertically before a deep dive.*

The harbour seal (Phoca vitulina) *can attain a weight of 100 kg on a diet mostly of fish and squid.*

Humpback whales breach the surface of the sea in a shower of foam.

Lazily stretched on rocks and boulders, seals bask in the sun.

The grey seal (Halichoerus grypus) *is the largest of Canadian seals; the male can weight up to 450 kg.*

The St. Lawrence bathes a succession of cities and picturesque coastal villages with evocative names that either bring events of the past to life or describe a geological feature, such as Les Éboulements, Percé, Cap-Chat, Trois-Rivières and Sept-Îles. Some reveal their aboriginal origin – Kamouraska, Natashquan, Québec, Tadoussac, Rimouski – others are derived from the names of pioneers of European settlement – Boucherville, Laval, Montmagny, Sorel. These human habitats, modest at first, were built on the riverbanks in a variety of surroundings: wetlands, forests of deciduous or evergreen trees, peat bogs, beaches, rocky coves and flood plains. Today, the most representative fragments of these priceless surroundings have been transformed into parks and reserves to protect the local flora and fauna. Concerned inhabitants, reconciled with northern wildlife, are watching over these oases for the benefit of all who wish to see our natural heritage grow stronger.

At first glance, the work of the St. Lawrence is lost in its vastness. After studying it for a while, one begins to appreciate the significant role the river played, and is still playing, in the evolution of its many regions, all graced with distinct and valuable natural attributes. Finally, a more penetrating examination reveals the physical and artistic detail, the striking life forms that are born from the amalgamation of the river, estuary and gulf with the munificent valleys and untamed shores of the coasts. Within this ample panorama, the countless manifestations of human resourcefulness share the limelight with an exuberant nature sustained by virtually inexhaustible elements. Let us recognize the importance of this river, remarkable in its immensity as much as its diverse attractions. Perhaps, tomorrow, the legend will read: To know the St. Lawrence is to know the world. The universe that it has created is expressed in its image – in the infinitely large as much as in the infinitely small – gigantic, yet balanced in its disproportion.

Les Escoumins nestles on the shores of the St. Lawrence Estuary.

A LAST *look*

Previous pages: A small boat awaits the opening of the next fishing season in Minganie.

The breathtaking landscape of Bic.

The austerity of the St. Lawrence is dissipated by the luxuriant islands that snuggle in the heart of the estuary.

Following pages: The red sandstone of the Îles-de-la-Madeleine follows the curving shores of the Gulf of St. Lawrence.

A rocky cliff near Percé.

A secluded trail leads straight to the St. Lawrence.

Following pages: A beautiful sunset fires up the north shore of the Gaspésie peninsula.

Glossary

Abyss: Great oceanic depth.

Alga(e): A vegetal devoid of roots and conducting vessels.

Amphibious: Living or spreading both on land and in water.

Amphipod: Small crustacean with a laterally compressed body.

Anaerobic: Without oxygen.

Arthropod: Phylum of invertebrate animals with segmented bodies and an external skeleton, i.e., insects, crustaceans, arachnids, etc.

Backswimmer: Pond insect with paddle-shaped legs that can inflict a painful bite.

Baleen: Hardened string found in two rows of plates attached along upper jaws of baleen whales used to filter water.

Barnacle: Small, sessile crustacean covered with white, calcareous plates, resembling a volcano.

Benthic: Related to or occurring at the bottom of a body of water (benthos).

Benthos: All organisms that live on or in the bottom of a body of water.

Bioluminescence: Light generated by certain bacteria, algae, crustaceans and fishes.

Biotic: Related to life or associated with the development of life.

Biotope: Restricted geographic area in which living beings are submitted to relatively constant or cyclic conditions.

Brackish: Somewhat salty.

Brittlestar: An echinoderm with flexible arms attached to a central disk.

Bryozoan: Phylum composed of mostly marine invertebrate animals living in colonies attached to algae, rocks or other hard substrates.

Calcareous: Of or containing calcium carbonate.

Caplin: Small marine fish, well known for rolling in the waves during breeding season.

Carapace: Hard, protective armour that covers the body of some animals.

Carnivorous: Flesh-eating.

Cephalopod: Swimming carnivorous marine mollusc with a head surrounded by long tentacles lined with suckers, i.e., squid, octopus.

Chiton: Marine mollusc with a shell made of overlapping plates that lives attached to rocks.

Cladoceran: Freshwater crustacean that swims using its second pair of antennae.

Clam: Edible bivalve mollusc that burrows into the soft sediment of coastal zones.

Cnidarian: Phylum comprised of invertebrate animals that bear stinging cells called nematocysts, i.e., hydras, hydrozoans, corals, jellyfishes and sea anemones.

Copepod: Tiny crustacean that lives in plankton.

Coral: Animal comprised of a colony of polyps, each bearing eight tentacles, belonging to the cnidarian phylum.

Crustacean: Arthropod with a chitinous calcareous carapace, i.e., crab, lobster, shrimp.

Ctenophore: Phylum of soft-bodied animals shaped like balloons, with or without tentacles and devoid of stinging cells.

Current: Flow of water.

Cyclops: One-eyed minute crustaceans, abundant in fresh water.

Cyperus: Grassy plants of the wetlands, i.e., sedge, bulrush.

Ebb tide: Lowering tide.

Echinoderm: Phylum of spiny, exclusively marine animals that comprises sea urchins, brittlestars, sea stars, sea cucumbers and feather stars.

Ecosystem: The whole formed by the living beings of an environment and the non-living elements on with they depend.

Eelgrass: Marine plant of cold and temperate waters.

Estuary: Semi-enclosed body of water spreading at the mouth of certain rivers, where fresh and salt water mix and tides are perceptible.

Flounder: A commercial flatfish.

Gamete: Male (spermatozoa) or female (oocyte) reproductive cell.

Gastropod: A type of mollusc that slides on a large ventral foot and usually bears a dorsal shell.

Gyre: Marine cyclonic current.

Habitat: Where an organism lives or the site in which individuals of a same population live.

Holothurian: Sea cucumber.

Hornwort: Aquatic plant, common between depths of one and eight metres.

Hydra: Small, freshwater animal of the cnidarian phylum that bears six to 10 tentacles.

Hydrozoan: Mostly colonial cnidarian that lives anchored to hard substrates.

Intertidal: Between the upper and lower tidal limits.

Invertebrate(s): All pluricellular animals that are devoid of a dorsal spine, i.e., insects, molluscs, echinoderms, crustaceans, worms, etc.

Isopod: Crustacean bearing seven pairs of legs, flattened dorsoventrally.

Jellyfish: Pelagic cnidarian, composed of a contractile umbel lined with stinging filaments.

Kelp: Large, brown algae of rocky shores that can measure several metres in length.

Krill: The whole formed by tiny marine crustaceans; the preferred food of many whales.

Larva(e): Juvenile form, distinct from the corresponding adults, that swims out of the egg.

Lichen: A composite plant organism made of algae and fungi, living on the ground, trees and rocks, where it forms mosslike carpets.

Limestone: Rock made of calcium carbonate.

Limpet: Mollusc with a single, cone-shaped shell, common along rocky shores.

Littoral: Contact zone between land and water, or an adjective referring to that zone.

Mayfly: Insect with four translucent wings. Numerous fishes eat the aquatic larvae of mayflies.

Medusa: See "Jellyfish."

Micrometre: Length unit equal to one millionth of a metre.

Mollusc: Phylum of soft-bodied animals, often shielded by a dorsal shell and bearing a muscular foot with which it moves.

Monolith: Rock monument.

Mussel: Edible bivalve mollusc, with a bluish shell, that lives attached to hard substrates.

Nudibranch: Marine gastropod with no external shell.

Nutriment: A nutritive substance that can be assimilated without having to be digested.

Old Capital: Designates the town of Québec.

Paleo-Indian: Related to an Indian culture from an anterior geologic age.

Pelagic: That swims or floats; associated with the open water.

Periwinkle: Small marine gastropod of rocky coasts; some species are edible.

Phytoplankton: Vegetal plankton.

Plankton: The whole composed of microscopic and macroscopic beings that float in the water and drift with the currents.

Polyp: Simple, sessile animal with tentacles that often forms colonies, i.e., coral polyp.

Pondweed: Small freshwater plant with pink flowers, native of Canada.

Population: A more or less isolated group of animals of the same species that live in a delimited biotope.

Predator: An animal that hunts to feed.

Proboscis: The flexible tube that comes out of the mouth of some molluscs, worms and other invertebrates.

Riparian: Of or on a riverbank or shore.

Rockweed: Brown algae that usually grow in the intertidal zone of rocky coasts.

Salinity: Proportion of dissolved elements, mostly chlorine and sodium, that is present in the water.

Scallop: Edible bivalve mollusc that lives on rocky or sandy bottoms.

Scud: Crustacean of the littoral that has a laterally flattened body.

Sea anemone: Flower-shaped animal belonging to the cnidarian phylum, with a soft body surrounded by tentacles, that lives attached to the substrate.

Sea cucumber: Elongated animal living on sea floors, close relative of sea urchins and sea stars, belonging to the echinoderm phylum.

Sea urchin: Marine animal with a calcareous skeleton, covered with spines. The most common of all echinoderms in the St. Lawrence.

Sedge: Wetland plant with sharp blades and a triangular stalk.

Sediment: Layer formed by the deposit of dissolved and suspended matter.

Sessile: Attached or cannot move easily.

Silt: Light and fertile soil made of detritic sedimentary rock.

Spartina: Generic name of numerous littoral plants.

Species: Subdivision of the genus that groups individuals born of common parents or that have similar features and that can successfully breed together.

Sponge: Phylum of primitive, sessile animals of various shapes.

Substrate: That which serves as a base, i.e., ocean floors, algae, wood pilings, etc.

Tidal pool: The hollow in the littoral zone in which water is trapped during low tide.

Tide: Cyclic rise and fall of the waters due to the attraction of the moon and the sun.

Tributary: A river, stream or brook that flows into another.

Tunicate: Bag-shaped marine invertebrate belonging to the chordate phylum.

Turbidity: The opaqueness or murkiness of a liquid.

UNESCO: United Nations Educational Scientific and Cultural Organization.

Water boatman: Thin insect with long posterior legs that are flattened for swimming.

Water mite: Small, floating arachnid living in plankton or among freshwater vegetation.

Water scorpion: Large aquatic insect that feeds on tadpoles and small fishes.

Whelk: Gastropod mollusc of the Atlantic coast.

Winkle (freshwater): Freshwater gastropod that mainly lives in ponds.

Zooplankton: Animal plankton.

Acknowledgements

First and foremost, we would like to thank our families for their generous and undying support, as well as the friends with whom we were able to rediscover – owing to their fresh look on the river, the estuary and the gulf – the inexhaustible riches of the St. Lawrence.

Our most sincere thanks also go to the people and the organizations that helped us explore the St. Lawrence and discover the wealth of its flora and fauna over the years: Patrice Poissant and the team at Tourisme Québec; Percy Mallet at Economic Development, Tourism and Culture of New Brunswick; Québec's regional tourist associations along the St. Lawrence; the parks and reserves of Lac Saint-François, Boucherville, Saguenay-Saint-Laurent, Bic, Forillon, Mingan and Bonaventure-et-du-Rocher-Percé; and the personnel of Bioparc de la Gaspésie, Randonnée nature des îles de Sorel, Zoo de Granby and Aquarium du Québec.

We are grateful to Marjorie Dunham-Landry for so efficiently assisting us in polishing the text. Finally, we thank Pascal Arseneau and Jacky Hébert of ATR Îles-de-la-Madeleine, and Léo-Guy de Repentigny and Philippe Fragnier of Canadian Wildlife Service, who willingly shared their photographic treasures to help us complete the illustration of this book.

About the authors

It was on the shores of the St. Lawrence Estuary, while pursuing Ph.D. studies in marine biology and oceanography, that Jean-François Hamel and Annie Mercier met. Guided by a common passion for nature, particularly aquatic life, they shared their scientific research and – why not? – united their destinies.

Authors of hundreds of scientific papers presented in congresses and published in international journals such as *Biological Bulletin*, *Ecology*, *Advances in Marine Biology*, *JEMBE*, *MEPS*, *Ophelia* and *Canadian Journal of Zoology*, Jean-François Hamel and Annie Mercier have made their main areas of study the underwater fauna of the St. Lawrence, as well as the reproduction and behaviour of various marine organisms and the effects of aquatic pollution on selected fauna and flora.

In more than 40 popular magazines from around the world, among them *Ocean Realm*, *Scuba World*, *Nature Canada*, *Discover Diving*, *Rodale's Scuba Diving*, *Géo Plein Air*, *FAMA*, *Récifal*, *Explore*, *Photo Life/Sélection*, *l'Escale Nautique* and *Quatre-Temps*, the authors have published some 250 articles on such topics as scuba diving, photography, wildlife, travel and environmental issues. Their knowledge of the complex universe of the St. Lawrence has also enabled them to make special contributions to the production of documentaries.

Their association, the Society for the Exploration and Valuing of the Environment (SEVE), founded in January 1995, is dedicated to the study and promotion of natural habitats around the globe through scientific research and photojournalism (www.seve.cjb.net).

Lithographed on Jenson 200 M paper
and printed in Canada at Interglobe Printing Inc.,
an affiliate of Transcontinental Printing Inc. in October 2000

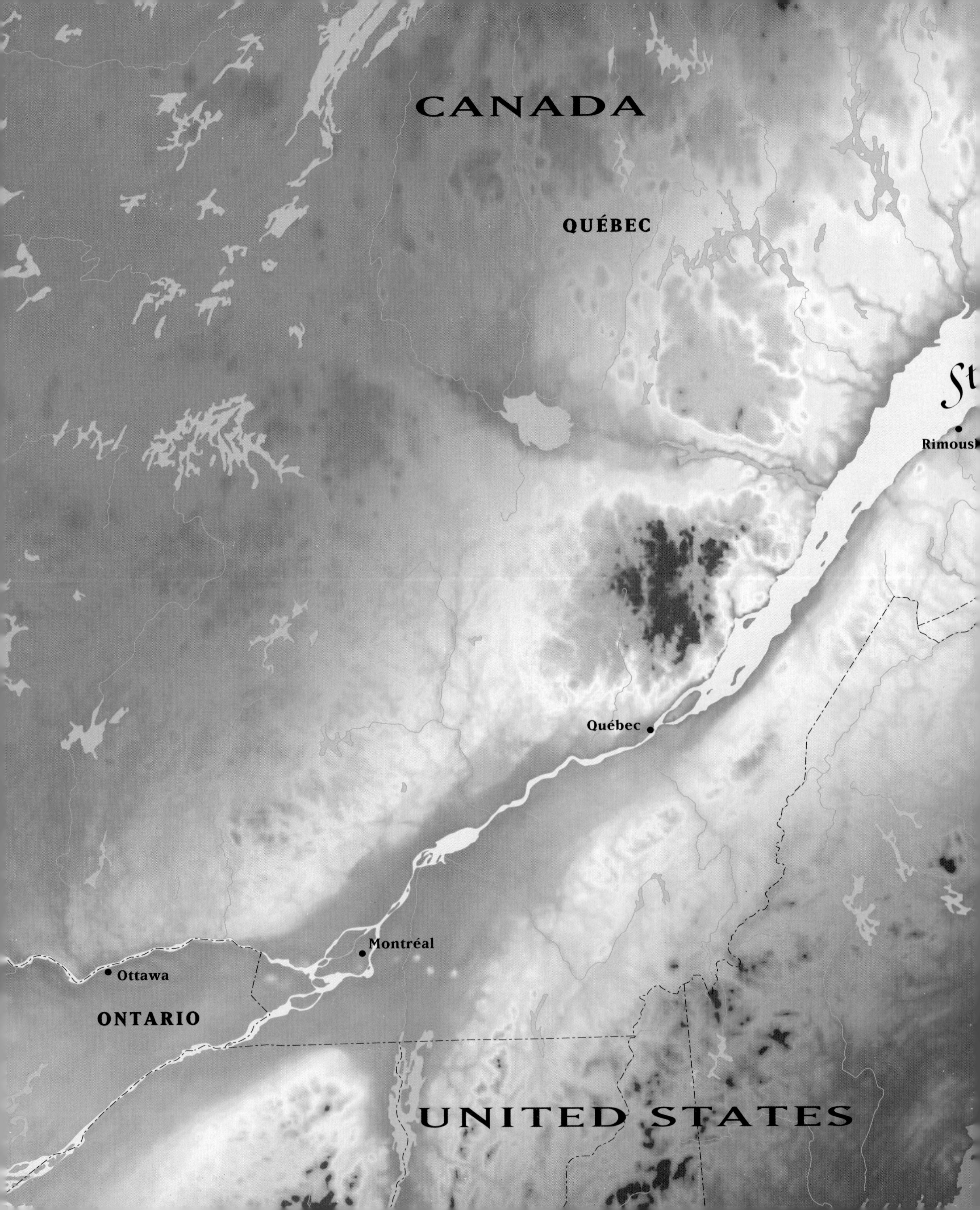

CANADA

QUÉBEC

St

Rimousk

Québec

Montréal

Ottawa

ONTARIO

UNITED STATES